Executive Focus

Your Life and Career

Also available from ASQ Quality Press:

The Executive Guide to Improvement and Change
G. Dennis Beecroft, Grace L. Duffy, and John W. Moran

The Quality Improvement Handbook, Second Edition
John E. Bauer, Grace L. Duffy, and Russell T. Westcott, editors

The Executive Guide to Understanding and Implementing Employee Engagement Programs: Expand Production Capacity, Increase Revenue, and Save Jobs
Pat Townsend and Joan Gebhardt

The Executive Guide to Understanding and Implementing Lean Six Sigma: The Financial Impact
Robert M. Meisel, Steven J. Babb, Steven F. Marsh, and James P. Schlichting

The Executive Guide to Understanding and Implementing Quality Cost Programs: Reduce Operating Expenses and Increase Revenue
Douglas C. Wood

The Executive Guide to Understanding and Implementing the Baldrige Criteria: Improve Revenue and Create Organizational Excellence
Denis Leonard and Mac McGuire

The Certified Manager of Quality/Organizational Excellence Handbook, Third Edition
Russell T. Westcott, editor

Mapping Work Processes, Second Edition
Bjørn Andersen, Tom Fagerhaug, Bjørnar Henriksen, and Lars E. Onsøyen

The Quality Toolbox, Second Edition
Nancy R. Tague

Lean Kaizen: A Simplified Approach to Process Improvements
George Alukal and Anthony Manos

Root Cause Analysis: Simplified Tools and Techniques, Second Edition
Bjørn Andersen and Tom Fagerhaug

Enabling Excellence: The Seven Elements Essential to Achieving Competitive Advantage
Timothy A. Pine

To request a complimentary catalog of ASQ Quality Press publications, call 800-248-1946, or visit our Web site at http://www.asq.org/quality-press.

Executive Focus

Your Life and Career

Grace L. Duffy and John W. Moran

ASQ Quality Press
Milwaukee, Wisconsin

American Society for Quality, Quality Press, Milwaukee, WI 53203
© 2009 by ASQ
All rights reserved. Published 2008.
Printed in the United States of America.

14 13 12 11 10 09 08   5 4 3 2 1

Library of Congress Cataloging-in-Publication Data

Duffy, Grace L.
 Executive focus : your life and career / Grace L. Duffy and John W. Moran.
   p. cm.
 Includes index.
 ISBN 978-0-87389-747-1
 1. Executive ability. 2. Executives. I. Moran, John W. II. Title.
 HD38.2.D84 2008
 658.4'09—dc22

                         2008037148

No part of this book may be reproduced in any form or by any means, electronic, mechanical, photocopying, recording, or otherwise, without the prior written permission of the publisher.

Publisher: William A. Tony
Acquisitions Editor: Matt T. Meinholz
Project Editor: Paul O'Mara
Production Administrator: Randall Benson

ASQ Mission: The American Society for Quality advances individual, organizational, and community excellence worldwide through learning, quality improvement, and knowledge exchange.

Attention Bookstores, Wholesalers, Schools, and Corporations: ASQ Quality Press books, videotapes, audiotapes, and software are available at quantity discounts with bulk purchases for business, educational, or instructional use. For information, please contact ASQ Quality Press at 800-248-1946, or write to ASQ Quality Press, P.O. Box 3005, Milwaukee, WI 53201-3005.

To place orders or to request a free copy of the ASQ Quality Press Publications Catalog, including ASQ membership information, call 800-248-1946. Visit our Web site at www.asq.org or http://www.asq.org/quality-press.

∞ Printed on acid-free paper

Library
University of Texas
at San Antonio

Quality Press
600 N. Plankinton Avenue
Milwaukee, Wisconsin 53203
Call toll free 800-248-1946
Fax 414-272-1734
www.asq.org
http://www.asq.org/quality-press
http://standardsgroup.asq.org
E-mail: authors@asq.org

Contents

Preface ix

Introduction xv

Chapter 1   Personal and Organizational Fog   1
   Sea Fog   1
   Doubt   4

Chapter 2   Homeland and Personal Security   9
   Being Alert   9
   How to Handle Them 10
   Gathering the Truth and Nothing But
      the Truth 13
   Using Organizational Data for
      Personal Security 17

Chapter 3   Communicating Decisions and Ideas .. 23
   Your Personal Vision SWOT 25
   Communicating Hard Decisions Versus Soft 27
   The Stress of Decisions and Ideas 29
   Make the Work Enjoyable 30
   Finding Your Right Spot 31

Chapter 4   Organizational Need 33
   Listening and Intelligence Data Gathering 34
   Has the Organization Improved Since I Joined? .. 38

      Is the Organization in the Place it Should
         be Today? 41
      Summary 43

Chapter 5 Personal and Organizational Clutter ... 45
      Eliminating Organizational Clutter 48
      Eliminating Personal Clutter 54
      Summing Up 56

Chapter 6 Organizational Momentum 59
      What Momentum Do You Create? 62
      What Did I Do to Reach this State? 63
      Kinetic Energy and Dark Energy 65
      Reward What You Want to Continue 66
      Employ Organizational and Personal
         Momentum 67

Chapter 7 Job and Place Mismatch 69
      Sound Advice 69
      How to Handle Repeated Trips to the
         Transition Zone 76

Chapter 8 Achievement and Avoidance Goals 79

Chapter 9 Sensory Indicators 89
      Measurement is Strength 89

Chapter 10 Managing Workforce Talent 101
      Current Workers 105
      Departing Workers 108
      Retiring Workers 108

**Chapter 11 Multi-Generational Teams Need
            Focus, Too 111**
      The New Team Makeup 112
      How to Build Effective Teams 113

Elements of Effective Teams	115
Technology and Teams	118
Behavior and Teams	119
Teams and Innovation	120

Chapter 12   Pause–Relax–Refresh **127**
Faster and Faster 127

Chapter 13   Summary: Now What? **135**
Now What? 135
Keeping Yourself Motivated and Engaged 137

Index *139*

Preface

- Do you ever feel stressed out?
- Do you feel as though you might be having a panic attack?
- Are you constantly in touch with your organization—by e-mail, phone, voicemail—at all hours of the day or night?
- Do you feel as though people are watching you do all the work?
- Are you the first one to arrive in the morning?
- Are you the last one to leave at night?
- Do you feel as though you are the only competent one in the organization?

If you answered "yes" to these questions, then you may have lost your Executive Focus and moved into Manure Management. Manure is good for feeding organizational growth. Manure works best, however, when it is spread across an entire field of operations, not when it is piled on the carpet in the corner office.

Executive Focus is written for the individual who leads an organization—the CEO, the senior manager of a major operating function, a department manager, or a senior technical contributor. It is for someone in a new organization, a new role, or a new position. It is also for someone who wants to refocus an existing role. For someone aspiring to one of those roles but not quite there yet, this book provides the tools, tips, and techniques that will focus a career plan.

The changes required to transition a successful entrepreneur into the effective executive of a complex enterprise are well documented in current business literature. The in-place senior executive needs a more subtle set of patterns with which to assess the options for continued personal success.

This book is written by executives for executives. We, the authors, have a combined 70 years as president, executive vice president, senior manager, and other leadership positions in which we have effectively charted the waters of personal success. Our intent is to share the observations, patterns, indicators, and decisions that have served us well over the past four decades.

How does the executive know that all is not perfect in paradise? We ask ourselves a series of questions in order to begin the journey of introspection. Some of these questions appear at the opening of this Preface.

Executive Focus is about:

- Keeping organization momentum going in the right direction
- Keeping the ship on course
- Looking for danger
- Making contingency plans
- Bringing balance to a professional and personal life
- Using creative leadership energy to take you where *you* want to go

This book is about what you know the organization needs from you, not about what you are currently doing. The focus of the book is about how to manage your business and your career so that they don't manage you. *Executive Focus* is about you, the executive, and the way you run an organization. It will help you avoid being part of an organization that runs you.

In the coming chapters we explore many of the work-life roadblocks that pop up from time to time to derail our Executive Focus Dark Energy[1] and channel it into areas that drain us mentally and physically. We offer solutions to overcome these roadblocks and refocus energy toward expanding your personal universe.

According to Booz Allen's *Strategy + Business* magazine, one-third of global executive successions in 2005 were performance related, senior executives forced to resign because of either poor performance or disagreements with the board. In 2005, North America experienced a record level of performance-related turnover: 35 percent of all departing senior execs left involuntarily. Europe, at 42 percent, experienced near-record levels in performance-driven departures. Asia-Pacific followed, with 28 percent of its senior executives leaving involuntarily. Japan's rate of forced turnover was 12 percent. Globally, only 51 percent of outgoing senior execs left office voluntarily. Successions resulting from mergers made up the difference.

For the purposes of the study, Booz Allen classified senior executive departures in one of three categories:

- **Merger-driven** The senior exec left after his or her company was acquired by or combined with another.

- **Performance-related** The senior exec was forced to resign because of either poor performance or disagreements with the board.

- **Regular transition** The senior exec made a well-planned and long-scheduled career move.

A July 2007 *Wall Street Journal* sidebar states that 35 percent of U.S. senior execs are uncomfortable about or feeling insecure in their positions. CNN's *Money* posited in 2005 that there are two major reasons for executive turnover. First, companies may be replacing senior executives who guided the company through recession with someone who can better lead it as the economic turnaround gains strength. "At this stage of the [economic] recovery it is not uncommon to see increased changes in leadership. A senior executive who was intended to keep the boat afloat during the recession may not be the best person to lead in times of accelerated growth," the article stated.

Second, as senior executive pay continues to soar, corporate boards expect better performance. "Those who fail to deliver will be asked to tender their resignation or risk being forced out in a shareholder revolt."

These quotes, written during the stock market boom of 2006 and 2007, acknowledge the required transition for executives from a recessionary leadership challenge to leadership in a galloping expansion period. The year 2007 saw a re-balance of the enterprise into a more long-term stance of asset allocation and strategic re-positioning. This transition creates another decision point in the executive's strategy to move a career forward using a new set of patterns.

Executive Focus provides you with the skills to anticipate and plan for changes in your personal or organizational career. A prepared executive can choose the next position rather than accept what's offered by the board or as part of an M&A agreement.

The "Executive" part of this title is about the total person in the job. It represents a combination of your skills, education, experience, knowledge, and proficiency. It is the way you have learned to manage your affairs, accomplish duties assigned to you, and handle power.

The "Focus" part of the title encompasses what you need to accomplish and how you interact with your subordinates and superiors in order to make clear a vision and the process needed to achieve it.

It is also about how you align your career with your skills, education, experience, knowledge, and proficiency, assuring that they are all in the right place in your life and aligned with your job duties. When this happens, you experience Executive

Focus. When Executive Focus is at its peak, you feel excited and in charge of your destiny and your organization's destiny.

Some say it is all about the work. Your life *is* your work. If this were not so, you would not be this far in your career. The balance of work and personal life is, however, still very important.

Executive Focus is not in your job description because no one has ever defined it for you. In essence, it is *your* expectation versus that of others.

Be careful how others define Executive Focus "for you." Others may have enough control within your environment to attempt to define it. You do not want to be running after someone else's definition of Executive Focus. Who in your environment might have enough influence to define your Executive Focus?

- The company (company culture)
- The media
- The industry
- Your customers
- Your Board
- Your CEO, if you are President
- Your functional director
- Your direct reports
- Your family

The goal of this book is to help make work enjoyable, not just for you but for those who work for you and for other stakeholders. We all want to be proud of who we work for. Our goal is to help you find your right spot, both short term and long term.

Introduction

- Do you like being in charge?
- Do you like responsibility?
- Are you able to motivate people to do a task well and on time?
- Do you know where you are going and when?

If you answered "yes" to these questions, then you have the Executive Focus needed to drive yourself forward in the world of work. You have your inner drive focused on the right things and have achieved a balance between your life and career. You have achieved something most people are striving to accomplish today. In this book we will help you fine tune your Executive Focus to get the desired balance between life and career that you are seeking.

EXECUTIVE FOCUS' INNER DRIVE

Executive Focus is the energy that powers your internal career guidance system. It is not an energy we can see but one that develops its power over time. Early on in your life you may have felt its presence when you took on leadership roles in school, college, sports, student government, or professional organizations. You may not have known of its power, but something was driving you to put your hand up and volunteer. You had the desire to be a leader.

The more leadership roles you achieved and accomplished successfully, the more you enjoyed the feeling and responsibilities of being a leader. These feelings were the power of the Executive Focus building up and gaining power and momentum within you.

Building the power of Executive Focus is a personal thing. It has to feel comfortable to you in order for the Executive Focus power to fuel you as a leader. We have all seen overbearing parents who push their children to be the leader or superstar in school or sports with disastrous results. If a person does not like the feeling of being the leader, then his or her Executive Focus diminishes over time. Executive Focus will eventually stabilize at a level where he or she feels most comfortable and in control of their destiny.

Everyone has this Executive Focus power but one key ingredient to really making it a powerful force within you is the want, desire, and drive to be a leader. Many people are quite content to be a follower and their Executive Focus operates at a low level. Every once in a while they may feel the desire to be the leader but realize they are not willing to put in the personal investment and commitment required to sustain the desire and role of a leader. However, like all guidance systems there are many factors that can throw your Executive Focus off course. We will discuss these course-altering factors and offer some tips to minimize their effects throughout this book.

EXECUTIVE FOCUS' DARK ENERGY

In today's scientific journals there are many discussions about dark energy, a repulsive force that opposes the self-attraction of matter and causes the expansion of the universe to accelerate. The concept of dark energy was first proposed, and then discarded, by Albert Einstein early in the 20th century.[2]

The search for dark energy was triggered by the discovery in 1998 of images from the Hubble Space Telescope of a distant supernova that implied an accelerating, expanding universe, which in turn required a new cosmological model. Although dark energy is predicted in particle physics, it has never been directly observed. It is generally agreed, however, that dark energy dominates the universe, which is projected to have a composition of 70 percent dark energy, 29.5 percent dark matter, and 0.5 percent bright stars. By 2006, astronomers using the space telescope to examine more distant supernovas had found evidence of the effects of dark energy dating to 9 billion years ago.

It is called "dark" because we don't directly see it. "Dark" is code for "we have absolutely no clue what it is." But scientists have determined that it makes up two-thirds of the universe.[3]

In this book we are going to help you unlock your Executive Focus' Dark Energy—the fuel that powers your internal career guidance system. Since the universe is estimated to be two-thirds dark energy, we will assume that you have the same amount. Finding and refocusing your dark energy will help you accelerate and expand your universe and provide you with a more enjoyable, less stressful, life.

Executive Focus' Inner Drive/Dark Energy is about:

- Keeping the organization's momentum going in the right direction.

- Keeping the organization and your career on course.

- Looking for danger and trusting your intuition. If it catches your attention, it is worth a second look.

- Making contingency plans for yourself and your organization.

- Bringing balance to your professional and personal life. Being honest with yourself.

- Using that extra 70 percent of your dark energy to get where YOU want to go.

Executive Focus is designed for those who lead an organization either as the head of or as a part of the organization. It is for those who are in a new organization, new role, or new position and those who want to refocus an existing role or position. *Executive Focus* is about what the organization needs you to do and not about what you are currently doing. The focus of this book is about you managing your business and career, and not letting them manage you. It is about unlocking your Executive Focus and developing its energy to energize your career and your career path.

May the Dark Energy be with you and ever-expanding.

Notes

1. Executive Energy Dark Focus – explained on page xv.
2. http://en.wikipedia.org/wiki/Dark_energy, – 74k – Jul 4, 2007
3. Ibid.

1
Personal and Organizational Fog

- Do you feel off-course in your career and life?
- Are you constantly being caught off guard?
- Are you unable to navigate in the new world of work?
- Do you feel overwhelmed by doubt about the future?

If you answered "yes" to these questions, then this chapter will help you begin to get your Executive Focus back. This will allow you to develop strategies and begin the process of achieving balance between your life and your career. The new world of work is difficult to navigate without the appropriate focus and strategy to achieve the goals you desire.

SEA FOG

Sea fog[1] is a phenomenon seen along coastal waters in the summertime. It appears when warm air above the sea is at a higher temperature than the sea itself. The air above the sea quickly cools and the water vapor it contains develops into the sea fog. You may have seen it while vacationing along the shore. Wind blowing in from the sea drives the sea fog onto the coast where it can linger for long periods of time. It may have ruined a portion of your vacation at one time. A wind shift or higher temperatures can make the fog disappear very quickly. In business, this fog reduces our ability to see what is happening around us, which can create dangerous situations.

At times we can develop an "Executive Focus Fog" in our careers. This results from a cooling down of our Executive Focus when it collides with an organization that is warming due to growth or other problems. We spend all our time on the organization's current needs and we forget about or put on hold our own Executive Focus. Very quickly days turn into weeks and weeks into months; when we emerge from the fog bank we realize that we have neglected our career focus for a long period of time. Change may have forced us into a transition zone from which we now must emerge. (Transition zones are discussed in Chapter 7.)

An Executive Focus fog bank reduces our ability to see what is happening around us. This can create a dangerous situation in which we may be caught off guard by a sudden emergency with long-term consequences for both our career and our organization. The important thing for us as executives is to keep ourselves alert. If we find ourselves going into a fog bank, we must try to keep a healthy balance between career needs and the needs of the organization.

When ships at sea go into a fog bank, they have instruments such as radar or GPS and a crew with seamanship skills to guide them. Good seamen use the sense of hearing in a fog bank to listen for noises that may indicate a buoy or another ship approaching. Executives need both measurement instruments and executive seamanship skills to guide them while in an Executive Focus fog bank. In Chapter 9 we will discuss in more detail the sensory executive skills that are needed in addition to a regular measurement program.

One factor that causes Executive Focus fog today is that we work and live in a world that increasingly runs on short-term relationships. We find short-term commitment in marriage, work, religion, and friendship. Because companies are merged or sold constantly, we no longer have the luxury of a long-term commitment to an employer. These short-term relationships and commitments cause us to be in a climate of constant change and upheaval. Because we are always in a short-term planning or reactionary mode in regard to career plans, we may lose focus on what our next steps should be.

Today, new workers entering the workforce have not had the experience of long-term commitments that their parents experienced in their work careers. They have not seen long-term commitments in their families or school lives. Family members may have been downsized or outsourced and teachers laid off because of budget problems. New workers come to realize that there are no guarantees in life. This environment is very different from the one in which the authors grew up. It used to be that parents and relatives went to work for an organization and were pretty much guaranteed that 40 years later they could retire, receive a pension, and live comfortably. We had family members who were living the good life in retirement because employers took care of them. There was trust on both sides of the management and labor equation. Even Social Security was a guarantee back then.

Today, everyone experiences this short-term relationship and commitment phenomenon. It also affects a company's ability to recruit and retain talented professionals. We have lost the trust relationship that once existed between employer and employee. The game plan for today's work force seems to be to get as much as you can as quickly as you can and move on. This short-term relationship and commitment phenomenon makes it easy for employees to shift jobs. They don't know anyone with a long-term organizational relationship and they have no personal experience working for an organization for long periods of time.

This fast-turnover society we live in can push us into an Executive Focus fog bank very quickly, because we or key employees can leave or be downsized at any time. These situations can cause an upheaval in career plans. The fast-turnover society brings with it a new set of pressures that reward short-term performance and short-term gain over long-term stability. The constant focus on short-term performance results never allows us any pressure release. Instead, the pressure is constantly on us to lose our personal Executive Focus. Today's status quo is to sacrifice long-term career goals for short-term organizational gains.

DOUBT

The thickness of a fog bank is a function of atmospheric pressure. The higher the pressure, the thicker the fog bank and the more our visibility is reduced. This reduced visibility keeps us always on guard for dangerous situations that could suddenly appear. When we have to be constantly on guard it causes an increase in our stress and tension levels. Throughout this book we will discuss various other topics that can create stressful situations for an executive. These can increase your internal atmospheric pressure and thus the thickness of your Executive Focus fog bank.

One of those internal atmospheric pressure building factors is doubt. Doubt is a feeling of uncomfortableness, uncertainty, or insecurity about an event, a person, or a situation. Doubt can be both personal and organizational. It can send us into a foggy condition.

Doubt can be a good thing. We all know that nothing is perfect and that there are always opportunities for derailment as we attempt to execute a plan or a recovery operation. One of the problems with doubt is that we may be frowned upon if we express it. No one wants to hear the sounds of doom or despair over the ability of a person or an organization executing a plan or project. We may feel that raising issues that cast doubt on the boss's plan will label us "not a team player." We may be ostracized for raining doubt on a major organizational initiative. No one wants to hear bad news, even when it is right.

We must be careful about how we raise doubt in public because we can be called on the carpet if it is not approached correctly. We have all experienced a situation in which we were blindsided when someone we thought we could trust raised major issues of doubt, in a very public forum, about a project we were about to implement. We were caught off guard and forced to scramble in order to get things back on track after such a direct hit on our credibility from someone we thought was on board 100 percent with the plan. In Chapter 2 we discuss the topic of Homeland and Personal Security, which addresses how we deal with internal terrorists who are lurking in the shadows, attempting to make us fail.

One long-term consequence of not expressing doubt is an increase in internal stress and tension. Because stress and tension increase internal atmospheric pressure, it is good policy to acknowledge doubt. It will improve your mental health.

It is also good policy to develop a positive mechanism to raise doubt in a public forum for major organizational issues. This allows everyone involved an opportunity to discuss issues they feel are not fully resolved or issues that could derail the project down the road. Acknowledging collective organizational doubt about a major initiative up front helps everyone feel that their issues were heard. This helps reduce stress and tension levels, and allows the organization to move forward more smoothly. Many times the issues raised in these public forums can be put to rest simply with information that was not available to everyone. Other times, issues may arise that no one thought of during the planning process. Doubt is always there; no plan is perfect and the conditions under which it is being implemented are always changing. On a regular basis we must continue to let those involved raise doubt issues so we can remain alert to changing conditions. If employees feel free to raise doubt in a positive way, they will keep you informed of things that are changing and will be able to focus their energy on the job rather than on suppressing feelings of doubt and leading the organizational ship astray.

We all know that keeping doubt bottled up inside, both organizational and personal, tends to cause stress. We need a vehicle that lets us acknowledge the doubt we are feeling. It is difficult to admit to ourselves that we are human and not perfect, and to admit that the organization may not be equipped to handle future situations the way it is currently organized. The approach we take to acknowledge doubt, whether privately or publicly, determines whether we are able to lower stress and tension levels. The best acknowledgement is a straightforward, honest assessment of the situation at hand, with alternate courses of action to rectify the doubt we are feeling.

To help us analyze doubt about an organizational issue, it is sometimes useful to use the doubt diagram shown in Figure 1.1.

There are two types of doubt: private and public.

Private doubts are internal concerns that should never be openly expressed.

- I doubt the organization is capable of making the changes necessary to survive in this rapidly changing market.
- I doubt the current workforce is capable of making the changes we must make to survive.
- I doubt we have the right product or service mix to compete effectively.

	Doubt	Worry level H M L	Reason	Whom to discuss with	How to overcome
Private					
Public					

Figure 1.1 Doubt diagram.

- I doubt our leadership has developed the right strategic plan.

Public doubt statements can be useful to challenge the organization.

- I doubt our competitors are that much farther ahead in new product development.
- I doubt that our quality improvement efforts are focused on the right areas to give us a competitive advantage.
- I doubt our customers feel that our service is excellent.
- I doubt our employees have the right skill mix to meet our changing market needs.

The doubt diagram is a useful tool for analyzing private and public doubt. It allows us to rank doubt levels from high to medium to low. Start with the high levels of doubt, listing the reason for the each and indicating with whom we should discuss this issue. It is important to raise each issue to the right audience. How might we overcome this doubt? For example, which training program will allow us to elevate workforce skills to the right level for competitive success? The doubt diagram walks us through all the worry levels so we are sure to cover each area as appropriate to assess risk and identify options for exploration. The doubt diagram keeps us from running off yelling "the sky is falling" without having the outline of a plan to put everything back in place.

Having the doubt diagram in place makes it easier to involve others in a constructive, rather than a destructive, dialogue about major issues that might compromise an important initiative. When doubt is raised constructively and in an organized manner, it is easier to get others involved and plan proactively to overcome it.

Throughout the remainder of this book we explore ways to keep an Executive Focus at all times. We must be vigilant even when we have made it to the top of our profession or have achieved all the career goals we set out to accomplish. It's easy to slip into an Executive Focus fog bank…and when the fog lifts, we can sometimes find ourselves way off course.

Note

1. http://en.wikipedia.org/wiki/Fog

2
Homeland and Personal Security

- Do you constantly feel uneasy at work?
- Do you feel unsupported by those above you and below you?
- Do you lack vital information to do your job?
- Do you feel that your organization is not aligned but disjointed?

If you answered "yes" to these questions, then you probably are working in an organization that has passive and aggressive personalities who derail meaningful organizational initiatives and who do not support you with tasks you attempt to accomplish. Dealing with these passive and aggressive personalities requires you to develop a personal security plan to help you keep your Executive Focus on track.

BEING ALERT

Since the September 11 terrorist attack, we as a nation have been on the alert for internal and external terrorists who would attack our country again. We have implemented counter-terrorist measures to warn us of an impending attack. To identify a potential terrorist we have developed watch lists to screen those who are trying to enter our country.

As with the United States, every organization has internal and external forces that want the organization to fail for a variety of selfish reasons.

HOW TO HANDLE THEM

Over the years the authors have encountered passive/aggressive types who would try to derail any meaningful organizational initiatives. Their motivation is usually to maintain the status quo, which benefits them personally. We have labeled these passive/aggressive types into the following categories:

The *Seniority Empowered* have been there through six presidents, four CEO's, and five reorganizations, have survived them all, and have not changed what they do and how they do it. Seniority is not a bad thing, but it does create built-in resistance. This resistance grows stronger as seniority increases and individuals develop a feeling of seniority empowerment. They have been in place so long that they feel they know what is best for the organization. In reality, they may have been out of touch for years with what the organization really needs because they have not been involved in any of the strategic initiatives. Over the years, they have lost their proficiency until today they are just barely knowledgeable about the organization's operations and current needs.

The Seniority Empowered will at times attempt to take over meetings where someone is trying to make change. The goal is to ensure that traditions with which they are comfortable are not forgotten, and that these traditions be preserved even when they are in direct conflict with needed change that others are trying to implement. They will attempt to derail any change initiatives by talking about the good old days until they wear down the other participants.

They will also engage others outside of meetings in order to "sell" their traditional point of view. At times they will successfully form coalitions to support the traditional view. They will develop these coalitions with anyone in order to keep the past alive. They tend to work with others in a positive way, and the out-of-date traditions live on, obstructing needed, meaningful change.

The Seniority Empowered is a difficult one to deal with but must be confronted if change is to happen. They must be confronted about their behavior and given a choice to change and join the team, move to a different job which will shake up their power base, or if they cannot change leave the organization.

The *Surfer* rides along the sea of change and always stays in the curl. Surfers are seen infrequently. When they appear, they are usually riding on top of the wave of change. Surfers have become masters of being at the right place at the right time with the right rhetoric. They attend all the meetings and trainings and even pretend to be making the changes required. In reality, they do nothing.

Surfers are masters of not actually participating in any change effort. They do not blatantly or publicly refuse to participate; they just don't. They are skilled at blending into the background and sometimes seem to be invisible. They often lack creativity and feel threatened by what is going on around them. They may make facial expressions that are intended to humor those who sit near them in a meeting, or they have themselves paged out of the meeting for some supposed emergency situation in their department. They know that overtly refusing to participate in a change effort will earn them an obstructionist label and they do not want to be viewed in that light.

The *Moray Eel* is the one who thought he should have had the promotion, should have been named the team leader or project manager, but he did not leave when he was passed over. The eel hides in its cave until you come close, and then lashes out to bite you and quickly retreats. You may think the eel is on your side, but he betrays you when you need him most and then disappears, ready to strike again when the time is right.

The Moray Eel is large. This is not the small hermit crab that steals the shell of some unsuspecting snail. This big green toothy monster can do real damage to the organization. Resentment grows as others are promoted. The eel looks for ways to create alliances among your direct reports in order to upset the balance of power during important decisions. Use the same tactic you would use on a bully: Confront the eel dead-on when you feel the bite coming from its lair. Don't be defensive. Instead be dryly factual about the attack that just happened. Use the facts of the situation to seal the mouth of the cave when the eel comes out. Once out in the light, the Moray Eel must learn to support you as the executive or move on.

The *Whale* is, unfortunately, a beached whale. A whale is the biggest obstacle to getting anything done in the organization. Whales usually hide behind the organization's policies and procedures to slow things down to a pace they can control. At meetings they attempt to derail any initiative that comes close to affecting their piece of the beach. They pretend to want change, but it quickly becomes obvious that they are buying time to set up more roadblocks. As we discussed in Chapter 1, these are the people who raise the doubt issue. Whether in public or private, they drop hints to anyone who will listen that the organization is on the wrong track, that the boss is making poor decisions, that the current change effort is going too fast, and so on. They use doubt as a weapon to derail any initiative that may affect them.

In meetings, whales try to stir up as much disagreement as possible in order to keep things in a state of disarray. They do not engage anyone outside the meeting for a private debate of points they disagree with. They want the public stage so they can point out the mistakes and failings of others. They enjoy belittling people and speaking to them in a condescending manner in order to build up their own egos.

Whales are masters of managing multiple disagreements at a meeting. Should someone try to expose them, they attack and attempt to make critics lose face in front of bosses. They have a finely honed reputation in the organization, so most people will not take them on. It is a losing battle.

The best way to deal with the Whale is to use the Doubt Diagram (Figure 1.1) and engage them in public to fill it in with you. Capture their doubts, force them to rate the strength of the doubt, and challenge them to come up with ways to overcome their doubts. It has been our experience that Whales usually rate their doubts as low and flounder when they have to come up with ways to overcome them. They dismiss them by saying, "I never thought they were that serious, but want to make sure they were considered." Once exposed they usually drop their objections and swim to deeper waters. You must be on guard since they regroup quickly and come back for another attack later to derail your project.

GATHERING THE TRUTH AND NOTHING BUT THE TRUTH

We have all heard the old saying, "Keep your friends close and your enemies closer." This is excellent advice to secure both your personal hearth and the halls of the organization.

The best way to keep the home fires burning brightly is to use evidence-based data to track performance you wish to target. Once you, the Board, and direct reports set the company strategic plan, identify targets for each major outcome required by your customers, stockholders, employees, regulators, and industry. This set of targets drives the measures with which you run your business. The current term for these measures is the *Balanced Scorecard*.

Imagine waking up and finding yourself driving in a car along a highway. You don't know where you are, let alone where you're going. You have no idea how long you've been on the road or how much longer your journey will take. In essence, this is analogous to a company operating daily without any sense of progress made (or lost) or of the strategic direction in which it is headed. A company must measure and report meaningful performance on a regular basis in order to drive operations towards a defined set of objectives.

Measuring and monitoring operational performance is of critical importance to an organization's strategic and fiscal well-being. It is also critical for you, as the senior executive. You want to be aware of what is going on around you. Surprises are *not* the executive's friend. The Balanced Scorecard concept has gained tremendous following, along with the more recent concept of "alignment," because the senior executive *must know with absolute clarity* what is going on within the organization and in the surrounding business environment. Not only is this important to the organization, it is valuable for everyone who wants to keep career options as open as possible for future growth.

When designed and implemented effectively, performance measurement provides the following benefits:

- It supports the organization's strategic plan by providing leaders with tangible indicators and goals that are relevant to their daily activities and those of the management team
- It provides executive management with sufficient and timely information about the effectiveness and efficiency of operations *before* significant financial impacts are experienced
- It creates a work environment that supports and rewards coordination and cooperation among and between departments and key functional areas in order to attain desired results
- It clarifies management and staff roles and responsibilities as they relate to driving expected performance and outcomes
- It drives change by focusing resources and shaping behaviors toward specific and tangible expectations and results
- It establishes a mechanism for assigning and enforcing accountability and for recognizing and rewarding outstanding performance

As a senior executive in the company, you are in the best position to know against what targets you and the organization will be judged. You are the one who is invited to the Chamber of Commerce banquet. You are the one who visits the most lucrative customers. But you are not the *only* one who should provide input to the measures assessing company performance.

Use all levels of the organization to identify the indicators that are most effective to gauge your progress to the goal.

All companies are familiar with the most common form of performance reporting: the creation of annual budgets and the production and review of periodic income statements and balance sheets. However, these traditional tools are not sufficient to monitor progress, identify issues, and drive behavioral change in a timely and effective manner. These are produced at a very high level and are not, for the most part, relevant to middle management or departmental staff daily activities. As a result, organizations require a second-level information source that synthesizes and summarizes the myriad of information that is available in today's business environment into a format that provides a "snapshot" view of the key departmental and functional trends and results. These can then be utilized to address deficiencies and develop action plans in order to stop or mitigate adverse operational impacts.

This second-level information source goes by many names and formats: the balanced scorecard, key performance indicators, and dashboard report card, among others. Regardless of the name, they all serve to satisfy an organization's need and desire for enhanced reporting, increased control and accountability, and improved financial results.

So what is a balanced scorecard? Whatever the format or name you use, it is basically a report card on the core business processes and functions that focuses on three key components, or perspectives, of performance:

- Historical-state performance information (baseline trends)
- Current-state performance levels
- Future-state performance goals/targets

Setting measures is a process of first identifying what is important and to whom. Much has been written about the "voice of the customer." New articles are now exploring the concepts of "voice of the process," "voice of the employee," and "voice of the industry." These "voices" are nothing more than distillations of requirements demanded of the company from different stakeholders. No doubt you have been part of strategic planning sessions where you analyzed customer and industry survey data in order to identify trends for market and operational competitiveness.

These inputs are the basis for establishing the balanced scorecard. The four or, at most, five major target measures are simply summary metrics of numerous sets of data gathered from within the divisions of the organization and surrounding suppliers, partners, and customers. They constitute a report card for the organization. The original four categories identified in the *Harvard Business Review* article are:

- Customers
- Financial
- Internal
- Innovation and learning

The internal measures are the ones most identified for "alignment" to the organizational goals you and your Board establish during strategic planning activities. These generally equate to the following areas:

- Cost effectiveness
- Staff productivity
- Process efficiency
- Cycle time

These measures are important only in as much as they specifically relate to meeting the major requirements of your customers. Measuring how quickly you rake the leaves on the front lawn may or may not be a useful measure to meet customer requirements for delivery of product in Abu Dhabi. Just because you can measure it does not mean it should be a part of the scorecard. Certainly, raking the leaves before they kill the grass is an important measure for the grounds department. That measure rolls up with many others until you have a final indicator of internal process performance.

Before proceeding it is important to note what a report card is and what it is not. A report card is a management tool intended to provide all levels of management and staff with an enhanced ability to monitor performance and progress, establish and maintain accountability and responsibility, reward superior results, identify operational deficiencies, and encourage appropriate behavior and actions toward common goals. It is not a replacement for other meaningful and necessary reporting mechanisms such as monthly financial statements or departmental-level operating reports. It is also not a panacea for a company's fiscal problems. A report card, in and of itself, will not be effective unless it is designed, implemented, and supported in an effective and consistent manner.

This report card can, however, support you as the executive in gluing your leadership team together toward a consistent vision of the organization. Having concrete data with which to address differences of opinion goes a long way toward holding the Surfers to a deliverable they would prefer to forget. Tangible performance data from the functional area led by the beached Whale clearly shows what has and has not been done, how well, and by what deadline.

USING ORGANIZATIONAL DATA FOR PERSONAL SECURITY

The authors developed a useful model for aligning strategic goals with the operational measures that are rolled up through organizational functions to the four critical measures recommended by Kaplan and Norton in their HBR article. Figure 2.1 illustrates the top-down flow of priorities, the operational level of working measures related to individual process performance, and the resultant summary of data back up through the management chain for effective decision making.

The executive leads the company vision and goal setting. It is important that you keep both the company and personal fit in mind when involved with this future focus for the organization. How you involve others in this activity will strongly flavor the culture and future landscape of your company.

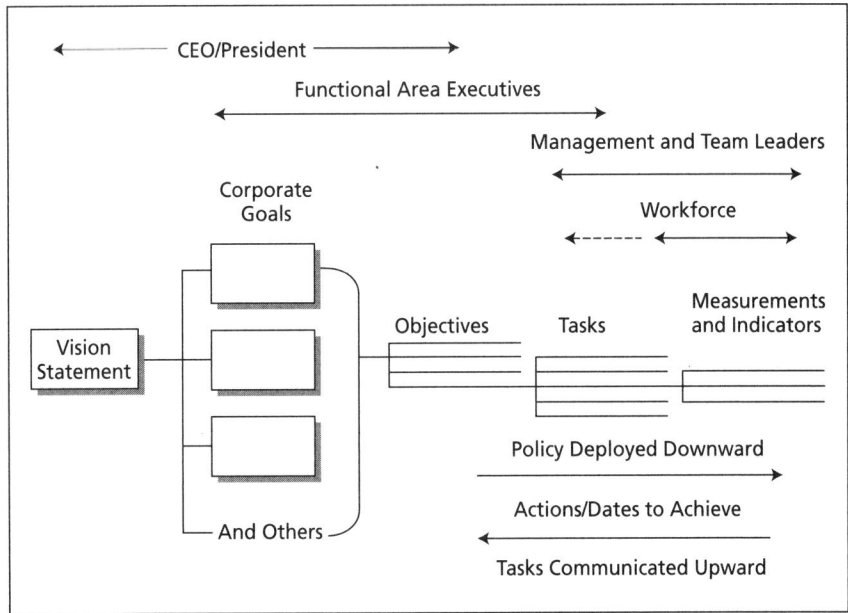

Figure 2.1 Aligning organizational goals and operational measures.

If the company is on a growth or restructuring path, you have many options for growth, both personal and organizational. If you have accepted responsibility for a maintenance strategy from the Board, you will have few options other than to build upon the path already established by the senior executive who charted the course. If your task is to downsize the organization you will have some options, but you will need to tread carefully in order to demonstrate the benefits of your strategy to all affected by your efforts. You will find more about these different future outcomes discussed in Chapter 4, Organizational Need.

Objectives, tasks, and measures/indicators are set as you have always set them. Involve those most closely associated with the process being monitored. Measure what truly indicates the effectiveness of the required outcomes as identified by the customers of the process, whether they are internal or external.

These measures come in many different forms, some of which may be:

- Hourly
- Daily
- Weekly
- Monthly
- Quarterly
- Yearly

For these measures to be useful, they must be quantitative and believable by those who are held accountable for their generation and application.

The purpose of using these measures for your Executive Focus is two-fold. First, your responsibility is to the organization that you lead. These indicators are crucial for the operational and strategic competitiveness of your company. Enough is written elsewhere about how to do this effectively.

The authors of this book are more interested in helping you use these measures to ensure your personal Executive Focus. That is the second purpose for using quantitative indicators of company performance. Your future is inextricably associated with the performance of the organization you lead. Use the corporate balanced scorecard as a personal watch-list of green-yellow-red career conditions.

When the indicator is on track for the company, ask how a positive outcome affects your personal vision. Do you want to use this success to leverage your position within the company and within the industry as a whole? If you are looking to move in the near future, will this success provide a springboard for you? Or will it create a golden chain forever associating you so closely with this industry or company that others may not see your value elsewhere?

If the indicators are trending to the negative, what may be the impact to your career? Certainly, none of us likes to see the numbers drop. But even in the best-run companies, for valid reasons they sometimes do. If the numbers are turning south because you took your eye off the ball, then address the issues quickly. No amount of resume gilding will hide poor leadership skills. If you are leading appropriately, then decide how you plan to use your actions surrounding this negative trend to show your talents as an executive in the face of adversity. Decide whether you choose to stay with the company and bring the numbers back into the positive and growing category, or whether you choose to set up the game plan for your leadership team and move on to another challenge that better fits your personal goals.

The success of Figure 2.1 comes from trusting your intuition. If something catches your attention, it is worth a second look. Watch the dynamics of those who report the organizational measures to you. The data is clear. Question how it is gathered. Question what the criteria are that generate the measures and the targets for minimum acceptable results. You can only trust the data when you trust where the data came from.

Table 2.1 is a suggestion for how to use organizational measures for personal Executive Focus. The Inner Sanctum label in Table 2.1 refers to those reporting most closely to you.

Table 2.1 Organizational measures useful for Executive Focus.

Hourly	Daily	Weekly	Monthly	Quarterly	(Semi)-Yearly
Yourself	Wall Street Journal	Key performance output variables	Internal indicators	Internal indicators	Industry
Inner sanctum	Market	Key performance input variables	Financials	Auditors	Board
	Exec assistants	Financials	Customers	HR climate	Regulatory
	Direct reports	Major customers	Employees	Financials	Financial
	Your health: Physical Mental Spiritual Social	Major competitors	Competition trends	Industry	
			Middle management	Innovation, R&D	

Chapter 3, Communicating Decisions and Ideas, offers a personal SWOT activity for identifying strengths, weaknesses, opportunities, and threats to your personal career path that come from your company or external forces affecting the organizational climate. Table 2.1 is a compilation of indicators generated through business activity that provide supporting data for assessing the soundness of your Executive Focus.

It takes courage to know yourself well enough to respond in a timely manner to important changes within your company and industry. It is far easier to watch the numbers in a general way and put wide-alert thresholds in place. Wide-alert thresholds are tempting because they allow us to turn our attention to other things without the constant surveillance required of top performing leaders. This is not a wise approach if you are serious about continued forward motion for your career or personal vision.

Homeland and Personal Security are your responsibility. As an executive, you are where the buck stops for the organization. As an individual with dreams and goals for yourself, you are the only one you can rely on to get there. Watch the future, watch the indicators, and watch your back.

3
Communicating Decisions and Ideas

- Do you feel like a juggler coordinating all your corporate priorities?
- Do you feel constantly called upon to provide "senior leadership commitment"?
- Do you struggle with keeping your employees informed?
- Do you get information from reliable sources to make decisions?

If you answered "yes" to these questions, then this chapter will help you focus on those leadership responsibilities that are critical to the success of your organization. How you set priorities, share information, and include others in decision making are strong indicators of effective leadership.

The buck stops with you. Any business book published in the past fifteen years champions the concept of senior management commitment and involvement. There is no way out of making critical decisions that will change the face of your company and, subsequently, your own future.

Most of us like it that way. We know what we are doing and exalt in assessing the situation, gathering ideas for alternative solutions, and deciding which path to take. Where we may differ from each other is how we do it.

As entrepreneurs in start-up or smaller organizations, we are called upon to generate ideas and make decisions on our own. There just isn't anyone else who knows the business like we do. Communicating our decision means sharing it with those who report to us, listening for their response, making slight modifications, validating consensus, and moving forward.

As our organization continues on its successful growth path, decisions become more complex. The entrepreneur must become a leader of others, not only of himself or herself. This transition from Lone Ranger to Corporate Leader is well documented in business literature. What is not often addressed is how the leader in that transition deals with the inevitable stress surrounding this change of major proportions. (Transition Zones is discussed in Chapter 7.)

Senior leadership work is focused on decisions, on recognizing the value of ideas within and outside of the organization. It does not matter so much where the ideas come from. What matters is how we use them. The executive is generally not involved in the simple, routine tasks governed by procedures or standards. The issues that bubble up to the top are the inherently complex, novel, or territorially volatile ones that, by their very nature, require deeper exploration, data gathering, and critical decision making.

As a senior leader, you already know it is impossible to sit in the corner office with the door closed all day making decisions. The business world continues whether we are ready for it or not. Unless we get out of the office and engage fully with our customers, employees, suppliers, and larger community, we will not have the required grasp on where the business needs to go.

Advanced preparation in business is invaluable to making good decisions under stress or when required to act quickly. Communicating those decisions also requires advanced thinking. To whom will you communicate those decisions? With whom do you make those decisions? Whose ideas do you elicit during the decision-making process? These questions are important to your personal and organizational success. We think of decision making as the province of great instinctive and charismatic leaders, but it is a learned skill that all must acquire and practice.

Decision making and information sharing have a social component as well as a technical component. With whom do you, the leader, share your deepest thoughts about running the business? Who is in your "inner circle"? When the employees of the company talk around the water cooler, do they know who has the ear of the boss? Are *you* comfortable with who is bringing you critical information with which to make decisions about your company's future?

One of the major social requirements of leadership is communicating the vision of the company. Since you are the top leader, that vision must also be your vision. Unless you can totally internalize the corporate vision as consistent with your own direction, there will be energy-draining conflict within you. Your Dark Energy will be siphoned off while dealing with this conflict, rather than being focused toward the needs of the business and your own career.

YOUR PERSONAL VISION SWOT

A useful tool for investigating any conflict between your personal vision and that of the corporation is the traditional SWOT (strengths, weaknesses, opportunities, and threats) exercise. This executive "SWOT on steroids" provides a structured way to look at the positive and negative drivers that influence your ability to gather, analyze, and synthesize ideas that come to you in the corner office. How you make decisions based on incoming information is a skill critical to choosing the right alternatives for the future of your company.

Schedule at least 30 minutes when you can shut the door and turn off the phones to conduct your personal-vision SWOT. On the desk, lay out four sheets of clean paper. Write your personal vision first and then your company vision underneath it on each piece of paper. Next, label the sheets Strengths, Weaknesses, Opportunities, and Threats. On the sheet labeled Strengths, quickly list all the good things about how your personal vision supports or is supported by the company vision. Do not take more than five minutes to do this. Next, on the paper marked Weaknesses, take five minutes to list any inconsistencies or risks apparent between your personal vision and that of the company.

Now, switch gears just a bit for the last two pages. Opportunities and Threats are external forces, just as Strengths and Weaknesses are internal. For the page marked Opportunities, write down any changes you foresee in the future of your company or organization that will positively impact your personal vision. Again, keep to the five-minute limit. You can do this multiple times, if you feel there are other thoughts just outside your grasp. Finally, take the remaining five minutes for the Threats page. What do you see coming down the corporate pike that will negatively impact or delay the advancement of your personal vision?

Once you have written on each of the four pages, sit up and take a deep breath. Do not attempt to resolve or even research anything you have written for at least 24 hours. Trust your subconscious to sort out the ideas a bit before you make any decisions on whether action is required as a result of your personal SWOT. Schedule time to revisit your SWOT writings within the next 72 hours. At this second session, identify which areas have the most benefit and the most risk for your career. Choose whether you wish to approach your leadership responsibilities in the company to maximize the benefits to your personal vision, or whether it is more appropriate to minimize the risks. Usually, if the company is tracking well to its vision and market, you will have more time to focus on the benefits to your personal vision. When the company needs your direct energies to short-circuit industry or market threats, the best approach is to focus clearly on corporate performance and, at best, minimize any damage the required decisions may cause to your personal future. With any luck, you are in a position to address a little of each.

COMMUNICATING HARD DECISIONS VERSUS SOFT

Communicating data-based decisions requires an approach that differs from communicating intuitive decisions. Although decision making is rarely, if ever, strictly separated into quantitative and qualitative aspects, when the announcement is made from your office there is usually a tipping point at which the outcome will be perceived as one or the other.

How senior leadership communicates decisions directly influences how those decisions are accepted by the receiver. It is imperative that we know our audience *before* we communicate our decisions. Much has been written recently about arrogance and humility in the executive suite. It is an interesting balance we must keep between being open to suggestions and confident in our ability to lead the organization.

Dr. Stephen R. Covey provides a useful suggestion for establishing an effective communicating environment: Seek first to understand, then to be understood *(The 7 Habits of Highly Effective People,* 1989). This approach is a good one. It helps minimize "snipers" who might use your communication for their own purposes. Knowing your audience provides valuable input; it allows you to tie all the different facets of a situation together so you can spin your leadership ideas back out to others in a personalized, innovative form. Understanding is the first step toward communicating effectively for organizational or individual success. Knowing the ground your words will fall on is important as you communicate decisions and ideas for personal growth and satisfaction.

Having your name on the brass plate in the executive suite means you have the responsibility to bring up the "unmentionables" at work. We all know they are floating in the ether just out of reach of normal conversation. *How do we get Jim to finally retire? Who will tell Madeline that it's inappropriate to yell at her management staff in the lunch room? No matter how well we write the annual report, we cannot change the fact that we did not break even last quarter. We don't have anything Marketing can get their arms around coming out of R&D*. Communicating "unmentionable" decisions and ideas is a core activity. Like most perishables, they usually do not get better with age. Use your personal energy effectively to determine the best time and place to put the unmentionable on the table. If it isn't part of the conversation, it can't be part of the action plan. Be selective about the time and place, but do it.

Certainly, there are strategic and tactical decisions that should cook a while as we validate operating data, complete staff training, or properly finalize legal documents before making any announcements. This does not mean that we are not addressing these topics within the appropriate group of involved parties, however. Chapter 2, Homeland and Personal Security, discusses the role of doubt and professional security. Sharing the decision-making process is one of those major areas where we must know our audience and know our selves, and where we must be sure we are clear about our purpose and with whom we share sensitive information, whether organizational or personal.

It is usually easier to support quantitative or "hard" data-based decisions than those made from intuitive judgment. Showing a control chart of a process or a trend chart of last quarter's sales data usually garners fewer questions than decisions based on softer, less tangible information sources. Either way, involving those who will be impacted by the decision in the data gathering and analysis phases usually goes a long way toward gaining consensus once the final presentation is made.

Sharing the decision-making load also helps to balance the stress of communicating the decision. Leverage the skills and talents of others as you scan your organizational or personal environment. Spend time during your quiet moments (and there are few of these, we know, at the top) to assess your direct reports, rising leaders, and personal contacts. Who do you want by your side for the long term? Who is useful for the length of a project and then a candidate for moving up or out? How do you keep connected with your family when you are pulled in so many directions at once? What information can you share about your business or your career that will solidify relationships that you can count on? The articles we read on employee involvement are also useful for family and peer involvement. Take advantage of the social status of being in the "in crowd." Use your leadership advantage to draw a core of trusted individuals into your inner circle so you can blow off steam or just share a new idea without fear of losing control of where that information goes.

THE STRESS OF DECISIONS AND IDEAS

Some stress is good. Most of us who rise to the top enjoy the challenge and are accustomed to high levels of stress. Each of us sets our own limit for how much stress we can manage for the long term. Balancing the physical, mental, social, and spiritual aspects of stress is a constant undercurrent during the executive day. Sharing ideas can be a time to regenerate our Dark Energy of mental strength while we reinforce a social contact. Many find that physical activity provides an opportunity to also strengthen the spiritual self. Learn your individual balance points and realize that they will change from situation to situation. The more you focus on your personal response to the leadership challenges you face, the more able you will be to adjust your stress levels appropriately to the situation.

Conflict encourages change; stress arises from conflict. Use change to gather information for decision making. Use the stresses surrounding change to encourage new ideas and innovative thought. Make it OK for your direct reports to share their ideas in a blame-free environment. Lead change where it best fits organizational goals and future competitiveness. Look for more about using change to encourage organizational momentum in Chapter 6.

The goal in effective leadership is to minimize bad stress and leverage good stress. Good stress comes from communicating decisions and ideas right the first time. Communication is a two-way street. As the leader, you are *not* a dictator. You are the gatekeeper. You are the catalyst who decides when to storm the next hill and who should lead the charge. Avoid creating the perception that you wield either the sword of power or a magic wand, expecting others to clean up the mess afterward. It is easy to allow our most trusted support staff to work incredible hours to create miracles of achievement. After all, we did that on our way up, did we not?

One myth is that you must never let them see you sweat. The downside to that approach is that the leader is under enough stress to do more with less. We are sorely tempted to accept the miracle and assume that there are more where it came from. Subconsciously, we know that is not the case. As the executive now, remember that your leadership team is doing exactly what you did to get ahead. Share the limelight. Acknowledge that your associates are churning out miracles. Include them in decision making and idea generation. Stress is minimized by a sense of confidence on the part of both parties. You are confident as the leader; put others at ease. That way, you will hear more of what you need to hear. Stay open to the war stories about how hard the battle was. Join in the celebration of the latest test of fire and be part of the team. You have already been handed the keys to the kingdom. Recognize the contributions of those around you.

MAKE THE WORK ENJOYABLE

One of the fun tasks of leadership is making work enjoyable. *Executive Focus* is written for you, the organizational leader. The authors' primary goal is to assist you in finding your place in the organization and in your personal world. Our experience has been that the executive sense of enjoyment is directly related to the enjoyment of those around us. Involving others in decisions surrounding new business opportunities, in securing new information for market development, or in establishing another rewarding customer relationship, is the basis of an effective workplace.

Likewise, knowing that the organization will continue to prosper after we have moved on to our next challenge is one of the rewards of successful leadership. There is little comfort in seeing the ship sink after we cast off in the last life boat. Most of us left the "I told you so" stage of our career long ago. A win-lose approach to management is rarely satisfying for long. The internal comfort of knowing that we have not only built a viable platform for our own career journey, but also provided a springboard for those around us, is truly rewarding. There are enough good jobs out there for everyone. Use your leadership position to help those who helped you. Involve your leadership team as closely as possible in the decision-making and idea-generating processes of running the business.

One of the authors had the pleasure to work for a manager who put his direct reports above himself as the organization was self-destructing so they would still have viable careers. He helped create opportunities for each of his senior managers to showcase their talents, skills, and abilities. He tolerated an uncomfortable transition assignment himself as a result of his efforts for his previous direct reports. His efforts were not forgotten by his former subordinates. Within a year, when his subordinates were secure in their new positions, they were able to help him re-establish his career. This illustrates the potential of a senior executive's ability to help others succeed as well as ourselves.

FINDING YOUR RIGHT SPOT

The responsibilities of the senior executive are advertised as strategic. In reality, the position holds a good deal of short-term decision making within the current setting. Preparing for the long-term is a moving target; our job is to scan the horizon for the best pathway for both ourselves and for our organizations.

Use your personal-vision SWOT as a reminder to support your own career while making the best decisions for the future of the company. Review your SWOT pages at least monthly, updating them as appropriate. Make the right decisions for the company first, then validate that the company's future is consistent with your own. If at some point you find that you and the organization are growing apart, start making plans for a smooth transition of power while you create another path for yourself.

4
Organizational Need

- Am I listening to the right people?
- Has the organization improved since I joined?
- Is the organization in the place it should be today?
- Do I feel the organization's future strategic direction is correct?

If you answered "yes" to these questions, then this chapter will help you build and maintain an effective information gathering network for career success. Monitoring, analyzing, and using information successfully are the life-blood of an organizational leader.

Our leadership success is all about knowing what the organization needs. How do we know what that is? Are my needs as an executive consistent with the needs of my organization? There is a continuous cycle of awareness that most of us intuitively generate within our sphere of consciousness. This keeps our internal monitors sampling the environment around us at all times.

Those new to the leadership suite may just be forming this internal monitoring system. The authors use the sequence of questions above whenever they are in a senior leadership position or supporting executives as external coaches. The questions are an excellent tool for navigating through Executive Focus fog.

LISTENING AND INTELLIGENCE DATA GATHERING

Top leadership rarely has too little input from others. The trick is to know what information is valuable and what should be put aside, either for later consideration or because it is not germane to the current situation. Sometimes it is easy to spot the "lobbyist" who attempts to foster a personal agenda by offering data to influence a major decision. Sometimes it is not so simple to separate the wheat from the chaff.

Building and maintaining trusting relationships with confidants, direct reports, councilors, and other providers of input for decision making is a major task for the leader. What questions should you ask to gather the appropriate information? What intuitive skills do you need to take the correct path for your future success?

Information comes from three basic areas (see Figure 4.1):

- Self
- Others
- Organizational operations

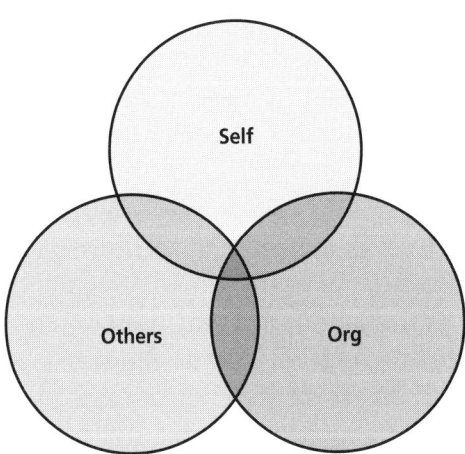

Figure 4.1 Sources of information for the executive.

The most commonly discussed information source is that of organizational operations. In current business literature this is often called, as mentioned previously, the balanced scorecard. This information is generated by the daily flow of transactions within the organization, among the different segments of our extended supply chain, and from broader environmental scans of potential market opportunities and threats. Most of us in the corner office are well aware of the major channels for this information and are already using these avenues for strategic, tactical, and operational planning and decision making.

External balanced scorecards are identified in Chapter 2, Homeland and Personal Security. There is also an internal sensory scorecard we leaders have learned to trust. This is described in Chapter 9, Sensory Indicators. Like the quantitative balanced scorecard, our internal sensory scorecard should take into consideration assessments of historical, current, and future indicators. Organizational operations are usually tracked by lagging indicators. We have hard data of what is happening or not happening within the organization. Once we move our attention to the future, we must consider more leading indicators. What indications must I see in order to be sure that I am on track for my personal and organizational success?

Extrapolating leading indicators into a useful view of the future requires us to use our intuitive or intellectual intelligence. Human beings are like radios—we take in broadcast signals from everywhere. Our ideas are multi-directional; they may go backward, forward, or through dimensional strata. When using our intuition, surprises are important, opportunity inevitable, and change certain.

Establishing our own style of gathering, assessing, and acting upon the organizational data is the easiest of the three input areas for the leader to put in place. There is usually a history of infrastructure and governance data within the company that we can tap into as we assume the top slot. Those who have been in leadership positions within the organization since before we arrived are available to provide and interpret the data while we labor to "get on board." As mentioned earlier, the trick is to know what of the guidance we receive is valuable and what comes with another agenda attached. This is where the other two areas of input become critical.

The executive does not get to be an executive without already knowing the *self*. We may not know ourselves completely, but we have a pretty good idea of our leadership style, of how we do business and how we best work with others. This book is written to help leaders assess the assumptions we have made about ourselves. How do we improve our ability to identify useful information, make effective decisions, and choose the correct path for the organization and for our own future success?

Senior leaders generally have a strong intuitive sense. Unlike facts, which presume a reliance on someone else's information, intuition is a direct experience that is self-evident and self-validating. It is either meaningful or it is not. Intuition is immensely valuable; many successful executives possess a high level of intuitive ability. More is shared on using intuition as an internal sensory scoreboard in Chapter 9.

The most challenging of the three sources of information is that coming from others. Where the organizational and environmental scanning information are generally quantitative, that coming from others is often qualitative. The intuition we use in assessing and interpreting information from self is instrumental in gauging the validity of the information coming from others.

To stay ahead of the pack, leaders must develop more curiosity and focus less on directing because it is easy to become isolated at the top. To fully assess information coming from others, we should do twice as much listening as we do talking. Leaders in the past claimed their positions through direct appointment of authority: We spoke, and people acted. Many of us who have been in senior leadership most of our careers have established leadership patterns that may not be as effective with a new generation of business professionals. Today's leaders still need to be in charge, but also need to listen and seek multiple inputs to expand their visions.

Most organizations today were built by and for baby boomers, and there is a growing disconnect between younger employees and senior management. The corporate clock is ticking and our store of available talent within the "boomer" pool is shrinking. Senior management must learn how to involve people of all ages in the continuous assessment and integration of new information into the decision-making process.

Active listening is important for involving others in the gathering and integration of new information. Listening is contact sport, not a validation of personal assumptions. Market research and survey results provide data, not loyalty. Customer and employee loyalty is built with face-to-face engagement. Solid working relationships are best supported with open dialog and honest sharing. If you listen with true openness, you might find yourself receiving customer honesty, not just feedback. Typically, when we ask for an evaluation we hear only from the extremely happy and the extremely angry. But if we ask customers or colleagues a problem-solving question such as, "If this were your company, how would you...," then peers are willing to help us serve them better.

Some of us came from the "Lone Ranger" school of management. We were taught that the executive must be decisive, tough, and willing to out-shout the competition. But behaviors such as abrasiveness, intensive brow-beating arrogance, and bullying often lead to the downfall of leaders. No other talent or ability can overcome this lapse in character. No combination of intelligence, hard work, business acumen, and administrative skill compensates for the lack of interpersonal skills. Being interpersonally inept inevitably sinks leaders.

We are often stunned by the number of people in management and leadership positions who lack basic social skills. When you talk to people, look them in the eye. Learn and use people's names. When conversing, say or do things that let the other person know you are listening. Do not dominate the conversation. Sincerely inquire about others' ideas and activities. Laugh at others' jokes and humor. Praise others' hard work and efforts in furthering a good cause. Smile when you meet people. These skills are basic for leading discussions designed to identify and resolve problems, for giving and receiving feedback, for coaching, making powerful presentations, and running effective meetings.

The ability to openly engage with others in a social setting is a sign of self-understanding. When we are comfortable with others, it usually means we are comfortable with ourselves. This body language message is critical for the senior leader. We must be secure in our own skin. We must have the confident image of a leader. Only when we appear open and available will others provide us with the information we need. When we transmit an image of "protectiveness" or "defense," others get the impression that we may be hiding something or seeking to present a false image for some reason.

The concept of *Customer Relationship Management* (CRM) is a useful model for developing an effective structure for judging the value of information that comes from others. Just as we would not trust input from someone we do not know in our personal lives, so also we do not usually trust information from unknown sources on the organizational level. Think about how you wish to be treated as a leader. Treat others the same way. Most of us went through the arrogance phase of leadership during which we "believed our own press." We may have felt we were more important than the other person in a conversation or thought that our ideas were the only ones worth considering. Usually, by the time we get into the corner office we have learned that we are just another one of the team. We have different responsibilities than others on the team, but we are all in this together. Create solid relationships with those you need information from on a regular basis. Establish verification channels for the sources you count on only occasionally. It is worth the time up front, before you must make fast decisions based on dubious information in the future.

HAS THE ORGANIZATION IMPROVED SINCE I JOINED?

As Kaplan and Norton suggest in *The Balanced Scorecard*, it is important to know the history of your organization. What are its roots? What traditions and myths exist that can either support or short-circuit the plans you will put in place for future growth? Usually your direct reports who have been with the company for a while are more than happy to share "how we do things around here." Again, listening is an excellent tool. You need not necessarily agree with everything you hear. It is valuable, however, to bide your time and gather information from available sources so you know what of the company culture is worth keeping and which sacred cows are ready to be barbequed.

Active listening is a useful tool. As executives, we need information about where we came from, where we are, and where we are going. This information is valuable not only to make decisions about the organization, but to guide our own personal growth curves. The authors use a five-step model for listening:

- Know the purpose
- Pay attention
- Interpret
- Evaluate
- Respond

Always know why you are listening and what you intend to do with the information. Certainly, we all use information for multiple reasons, but it helps to have a primary focus so we can categorize the data appropriately for the current situation. We can re-sort the input later for different analyses. Listening is an active verb. If we want information, we must pay attention. Too often we try to do two or more things at once and realize too late that some rare tidbit of information just flew by our consciousness before we could accurately interpret it. See Table 4.1 for suggestions that will help you address barriers to effective listening.

As seasoned leaders, we are already experts at assessing and interpreting information. As a new executive in an organization,

Table 4.1 Barriers and solutions to effective listening.

The Steps	The Barriers	The Solution(s)
Know the purpose	Unclear or lack of purpose	Define the purpose (ASK!)
Pay attention	Distractions Cannot hear	Eliminate distractions Focus on speaker
Interpret	Word meanings	Clarify
	Emotional hot buttons	Identify
		Develop behaviors to control
	Sub-verbal (tone, pitch, rate, volume)	Identify
	Non-verbal (body language)	Identify
Evaluate	Lack of facts/sense	Ask questions/clarify
	Incomplete information	Request more information
	Consequences	Identify
Respond	Any and all of the above	Give immediate feedback
		Acknowledge speaker's feelings

we may wish to elicit other opinions and interpretations as well. We still may go with our own intuition or fact-based decision, but at least we have respected the ideas of our colleagues and kept an open mind. Evaluation and response is an iterative cycle. We may repeat back what we have heard about an organizational issue in order to verify that we have interpreted it accurately. Involving others in the discussion builds relationships, establishes trust, and provides additional perspectives on the situation. Working with your leadership team on an appropriate response to a situation gives them a chance to know you better and to see how you may make future decisions. Table 4.1 provides a breakdown of the steps for active listening along with some stumbling blocks and solutions we may encounter during each step.

IS THE ORGANIZATION IN THE PLACE IT SHOULD BE TODAY?

Before we can fully envision where the organization needs to go, we must have an accurate image of where we are now. What has happened within the organization since you took over as senior leader? Is it getting better? Is the situation stagnant, just waiting for you to take the reigns to lead it in a new direction? Or, worse yet, has the situation deteriorated since you arrived?

This current state study is nothing we have not already done in other organizations. If yours is a publicly traded company, review the market reports; do not just rely on internally generated data. Get perspectives from inside and outside the organization. You probably did a good bit of research on the company before you accepted the offer to step into your leadership position.

Now that you have accepted the position and are closer to the action, review the data again through your new filters. Question any original assumptions you made about your approach to leading the organization to the next level. Re-think the role you expected to play as organizational leader. Are you still as positive about your ability to move the organization into the future? What additional skills, resources, and energy do you need to get the organization moving in the right direction? Do you feel the organization's future strategic direction is correct? What are the three or four things the organization needs? Experience shows that there are only a few options for where we should "go" with the organization:

1. Cleaned up/reorganized
2. Maintained
3. Grown
4. Downsized

How do you know which path to take? Evidenced-based decision making is useful as a systematic review. Chapter 2,

Homeland and Personal Security, introduced a number of approaches and quantitative indicators for environmental scanning, organizational assessment, and personal goal setting. As senior leaders, we are always on the lookout for information about cost and operational performance. Our challenge is to maintain perspective of the decision that is to be made. It is a personal decision based upon the factors involved with being a senior leader of the organization.

Failing to believe information that is staring you in the face is one of the most common causes of catastrophe. It is easy to get caught up in gathering information. At some point we must cut off the inward flow of data and move into the analysis and decision-making phase. Scan a combination of search databases, e-newsletters, Google, observations, business periodicals, and business best-sellers for techniques your peers use as input. Most top leaders have accumulated a sizable "executive library" by the time we take over the corner office. Remember why you kept the references you have reverently packed and unpacked over that series of moves up the career ladder. They are a good mirror into your executive soul. Use the information again.

If the organization is viable in its current incarnation, take advantage of your new leadership position to re-assess and marshal the troops for improvement activities. Numerous business models are available for this journey. The authors are partial to the "Core Process Redesign" 5-step model.[1] The organization undoubtedly has a number of improvement activities going on concurrently. Review the status of each project, assess, adjust, and implement.

You may have been asked to take over the helm as a result of major restructuring by previous leadership. In this case, the Board may be looking for you to settle down the waves and let sanity return to the rank and file. If this is the case, establish a maintenance strategy. Use approaches to stabilize processes, provide postponed learning opportunities for the staff, document successful projects, and reinforce the new culture your predecessor established. Although this strategy sounds like the most pleasant of the options, it is often the most uncomfortable for an established leader. We are accustomed to leading the charge, not serving as caretaker for the last administration. Be very sure you are ready to rest on your laurels, if this is the responsibility the organization has handed you.

Growing the organization is the most fun. This is the winner's circle. You will have lots of help discovering ways to re-invest in an expanding market. Remember to keep sight of your own goals while you carve out a new existence for the company. Never hold back the company simply because its future may not hold a good position for you. Take the company where the market will allow it to go. Better yet, build a market into which the company can take flight and soar. Your reputation will fly on the same wings. Once you have climbed the golden staircase, you will have more personal options available than ever before.

The most painful decision for the future is downsizing. Most of us have been party to these contractions as middle managers and know the disruption downsizing creates. If you are ready to lead the organization into the fray, gird up your loins and address the requirement openly with your Board and direct reports. Structure the downsizing in a way that shows Wall Street, your employees, and the community that you are doing what must be done in the most effective and humane way possible. Your resume depends on designing and implementing a surgical success with minimal scars to the resulting organization and its stakeholders.

SUMMARY

Regardless of where the organization goes in the future, ask yourself these questions:

- Am I the right person to lead where we decide to go?
- Am I still the right person for the job?

Ask these questions of yourself first; then open up the discussion to others within your intimate circle of contacts: family, peers, favored customers, community, Wall Street, social connections, and so on. Beware of losing the focus on *you* as the leader versus the organization as in a normal strategic planning exercise. There is a different reason for this personal environmental scan. As discussed in Chapter 2, Homeland and Personal Security, it is good to question assumptions. It is dangerous, however, to openly express doubt unless you know exactly what another will do with the confidence you share.

Maintain a balance among your consideration of organizational needs, your chosen place in life, and the type of job you want in the future. At this point in your career, this is not a simple discussion with your Vice President of Human Resources. Human Resources is focused downward into the competencies of the organization as a system; you must be focused up toward a personal growth path that very possibly does not include the current company's future.

Do not obsess over these decisions to the point of paralysis. It is important to relax and let the ideas come to us without undue stress from external stimuli. Walk on the beach, take a cruise, or visit a cabin in the woods. Ask "what if" questions and do not concern yourself with the "yes, but" answers that confound our creative thoughts. You have made these types of decisions before, although in less lofty positions. Trust yourself; believe in your intuition. Gather the data, discuss it with your inner circle, and be ready to move when the time is right. The organization will be better for your honest deliberations.

Note

1. Beecroft, Duffy, Moran; *The Executive Guide to Improvement and Change,* 2002, Quality Press.

5
Personal and Organizational Clutter

- Does everything seem to fall on your shoulders at the same time?
- Do you ever wonder what to do with all the "stuff" in your office?
- Do unnecessary disruptions sap your "Dark Energy"?
- Do you ever dream of restructuring your organization so people can really communicate?

If you answered "yes" to these questions, then this chapter will help you identify those items in your life that take up space but provide no value to your efforts. These non-value items can be both tangible and intangible. They can be files, ideas, habits, or relationships.

Organizational clutter: those things that get in the way of you doing your job effectively and things that impede the organization from moving forward and making progress. Chapter 2, Homeland and Personal Security, already introduced you to various manager types (the Seniority Empowered, the Surfer, the Moray Eel, and the Whale) who eat up resources, stall forward motion, and drain your Dark Energy.

Every year as part of your Executive Focus you must have a yard sale and get rid of those things that are in the way and no longer needed. Just as you clean your files or your house as you move on in life, so it is in organizations. As organizations evolve, things must go. Too often those things just hang on, or are rearranged to make the unneeded more efficient. This is not about rearranging clutter; it is about sending it to the landfill. Get rid of it. No three-month study is needed. It's obvious when something has outlived it usefulness and mission.

Clutter accumulates at all levels of the organization. Your Vice President of Quality uses the term *lean* to talk about eliminating clutter. Another term you may hear is *noise*. Noise is a term statisticians use to describe unexpected disruption in processes. Clutter is the equivalent of extraneous noise. Reducing clutter reduces the noise in our organization and in our life. Part of reducing clutter is getting to the essence of our working and living environment. You can cultivate essence by engaging in a few minutes of daily meditation to quiet your mind. And you can call on your essence in a tough situation by taking a moment to stop and connect mentally to that calm center of creativity within, or by inwardly stepping back from the action and checking in with what's most important to you before making a decision and moving forward.

Kevin Cashman, CEO of Leadersource, talks about essence: "Like flashes of intuitive insight, the awareness of essence comes to us through the practice of pause. It appears in the silence between our thoughts, the space between the problems and analyses. A parallel is the third law of thermodynamics: As activity lessens, order increases. When we pause, the mind settles, expands, and becomes more powerful and orderly. As a result, we can go beyond the individual issues, combine seemingly unrelated variables, and come up with new solutions or perspectives." There is more about Pause, Refresh, and Re-Focus in Chapter 12 of this book.

Reducing clutter allows us to find our organizational or personal essence and focus on what is important. We focus our Dark Energy on the high-priority items in the workplace and in our career. You probably remember your first line manager training: "If in doubt, throw it out." When you take over a new position, ignore most of what is in your inbox and see who asks for it again. Be somewhat cautious; because you are the senior leader, others are waiting for *you* to ask for information. The executive assistant or senior administrative specialist is an excellent resource for identifying critical reports, meetings, and so on.

Where do you start reducing the clutter? That answer depends on how you run your organization. Do you start with strategic plans and cascade ideas and policies down through the organization? Or do you observe the daily activities of individuals and departments, searching for things that do not add value to the total system that is your business? There is no one right answer to these questions. If your corporate culture is built from the top down, with strategic plans driving future action, then eliminate clutter the same way. If your company is more comfortable starting at the task level to identify future requirements, then implement your clutter campaign from the bottom up.

The concept of alignment is helpful in starting your clutter campaign. Figure 2.1 in Chapter 2, Homeland and Personal Security, describes the concept of alignment in terms of traditional reporting hierarchies. The executive team sets the mission, vision, and goals of the organization. Middle management translates the goals into objectives and overlays those objectives into the functional areas of the corporation. First-line management implements processes and measures to accomplish the activities and achieve immediate results to meet customer needs. Measures of activity and results are rolled back up the hierarchy for assessment, adjustment, and long-term planning. Everything that happens in your company and in the actions of your suppliers and customers related to your operations should be totally aligned to the goals and objectives you and your direct reports establish. Anything that cannot be tied to a specific customer or organizational requirement is extraneous. It is a waste of your resources.

Figure 5.1, "Personal and Organizational Clutter Matrix," allows you to identify clutter areas, both personal and organizational. Before you can eliminate clutter, you must

Clutter Areas	Identify	In my control	Outside my control
Personal			
Organizational			
Additional			

Figure 5.1 Personal and organizational clutter matrix.

determine whether the identified area is within or outside your control. Those areas within your control can be addressed immediately. You may need to involve others for those outside of your control. Use your influence to encourage others to use their control to address these identified clutter areas.

ELIMINATING ORGANIZATIONAL CLUTTER

When initiating a clutter campaign, it's important to involve individuals at all levels. Your leadership team is a critical part of the clutter campaign. They are the first wave of alignment. All processes within your organization come up through them to your office. As you follow the organization into the middle management and first-line operations, the opportunities for reducing clutter become very specific. Once your team has a clear vision of how to align all resources to meet some customer requirement or another, you are ready to start reducing the clutter that is in the way of your goal.

Figure 5.2 provides a vertical view of a generic organization. Compare this to Figure 2.1, which uses a similar approach on a horizontal plane to show the flow across an entire organization.

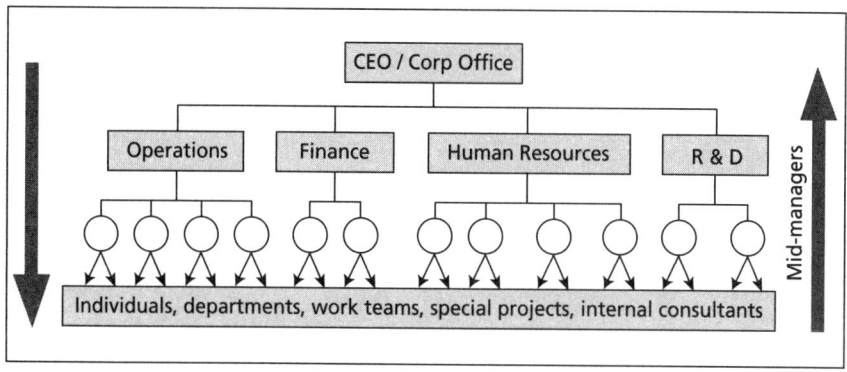

Figure 5.2 Organizational clutter top down, bottom up.

If you have not yet documented the goals, objectives, tasks, activities, and measures required to meet customer needs, do that before starting to "clean the closets." Unless you know what your business is supposed to do, you will not be able to align resources to those requirements.

What needs to be looked at? There is an entire body of knowledge available on the topic of organizing the company for maximum effectiveness. Business Process Management (BPM) is a family of processes and tools used to support the executive team in designing and implementing an integrated systems approach for maximum competitive advantage. BPM is an excellent approach for designing the structure of your organization to mirror the requirements of your strategic plan, vision, and goals.

To implement a top-down approach, first look at the integrated operation of the complete organization including your supply chain. Where can you reduce the use of resources while maintaining or improving the quality of products and services? A hierarchical list of opportunities might include:

- Organizational structure
- Business units
- Functions
- Product lines

- Traditions
- Standards
- Policies
- Processes
- Procedures
- Forms
- People
- And so on

If your company culture is more comfortable with the bottom-up approach, then begin with day-to-day forms, procedures, and policies and work up into the more complex opportunities as you realize the operational benefits of maximizing resources. Have a "clean out the Pendaflex day" in each of your departments. Pendaflex is a brand name for the hanging folders in our desks that hold the manila files where we store our informational treasures. What has been hanging around forever serving no purpose? What organizational boxes are your employees walking around that no one owns anymore? What information should go to long-term storage based on archival requirements? What is in storage now with an expiration date that has come and gone? How many earlier editions are on the shelf right next to the latest copy? When was the last time someone cleaned out the refrigerator in the break room? Most of us already know where the clutter is. We are usually willing to come in on a Saturday to clean up because we know it will be easier for all of us without all the garbage interfering with doing the job. If you must pay overtime to get the clutter out of the way, consider it money well spent. You will recover the time and more just by reducing disruptions.

The area that should be considered last is eliminating people. Involving everyone in the crusade to reduce clutter is important. The person doing the job knows what it takes better than anyone. When people know they are making the workplace safer, more productive, or more comfortable, they are strongly motivated to be involved. If we start the process by eliminating people, those who remain quickly get the message that the whole exercise is simply to cut headcount. Little productive effort will be placed on the task after that.

The most effective approach is to announce that no one will be removed from the company for some period, usually 6 months, as a result of the clutter campaign. Success stories are written about how individuals whose job are reorganized or eliminated by removing unnecessary activity are successfully retrained or re-missioned within the organization. Both of the authors have successfully used the techniques of attrition, re-training, temporary assignment, and good management communication to better balance headcount within organizations. By the time you accept the reins of leadership, you will be well acquainted with these techniques.

The authors are not naïve enough to believe that all employees will fit into the new organization format. In reality, employees and managers who should have moved on long ago are sometimes retained. Chapter 2, Homeland and Personal Security, addresses some of those individuals. Removing clutter does not replace the normal function of job descriptions, supervisory activity, and employee accountability and responsibility. In fact, the clutter campaign is a good time to refresh the focus of your performance planning and evaluation process. Inaccurate employee appraisals and feedback are a huge waste of resources; they become low-hanging fruit for Human Resources and line management.

Not everything must be thrown away; some things may simply be dusted off and recycled. As you work with your direct reports and all members of the organization, allocate unnecessary items to the best possible use. Some examples may be:

- *Landfill:* Be heartless. If a process, activity, form, or meeting cannot be tied to some valuable outcome required by a customer, internal operation, industry regulation, or special project, get rid of it. All it does is get in the way of the good stuff.
- *Hand-me-down:* If the item or practice is valuable but in the wrong place, put it to better use elsewhere. Create

a Goodwill Industries box within your department where these treasures can be recycled and tracked.

- *Share:* You may find items that are really useful where they are. Maybe they can support required outcomes in other parts of the organization, too.

- *Feng Shui:* The business term for this interior decorating magic is Value-Stream Mapping. Basically, it is the concept of identifying the best way to use resources within a process in order to maximize the outcome and minimize waste. How can you rearrange what you do to create the shortest distance from here to there?

- *Silver polish & put back up front:* Closely related to Feng Shui, this approach recognizes the value of what is already in place. Spit-shine existing processes and resources to make them up to date, and train the right people to take optimum advantage of them.

- *5S:* This Lean Enterprise tool is helpful for reducing clutter. There is more detail on this practice below.

Cascade the clutter brigade through the organization, top down and bottom up. Partner with the Quality office. They are experts at what the industry calls *lean* and a nifty little practice called *5S*, a set of simple rules for reducing organizational clutter that comes from the Lean Enterprise model. Based on Japanese words that begin with S, it focuses on effective workplace organization and standardized work procedures. The 5S tool simplifies the work environment and reduces waste and non-value activity while improving the effectiveness and safety of operations.

The five S concepts are:

- Sort *(Seiri)* — Eliminate unnecessary items from the workplace.

- Set In Order *(Seiton)* — Employ efficient and effective storage methods.

- Shine *(Seiso)* — Thoroughly clean the work area.

- Standardize *(Seiketsu)* — Involve your employees to participate in the development of standards for how work is done.

- Sustain *(Shitsuke)* — Resist the tendency to return to the status quo and the comfort zone of the old ways. Focus on defining a new status quo and standard of workplace organization.

Eliminating extraneous clutter gives us the ability to "notice" wisely. This ability is often based on knowledge, experience, and training. People want to make wise decisions that lead to appropriate actions. When our vision is cluttered with disruptions, we are not able to see clearly to our goal. We are constantly interrupted by side considerations that pull us away from the primary path. Once processes and procedures are defined, provide a system by which all affected employees are trained on the new systems and able to maintain and improve them for the long term.

Your responsibility as the executive is to make a complex set of tasks simpler by offering and encouraging:

- Pliable structures
- Simple rules and systems
- Independent action by the individual

These characteristics are part of the Business Process Management work. It is critical to build organizational structures that support individual innovation while maintaining a consistent and reliable product or service. As employees and managers clear out the clutter and focus on what is really important to meet customer needs, each individual is better able to make effective decisions.

Real leaders handle their own dirty work. You will want to be visible reducing clutter in your communications, meetings, planning, and other activities you lead within the organization. Leaders who expect others to rework ineffective practices or dismiss subordinates rarely earn the same credibility and trust as those who courageously do their own dirty work. One of the authors helped redesign a major portion of a Fortune 100 corporation only to see the new CEO gut one-third of available office space in order to create a white-carpeted, palatial office suite for himself. His excuse was that he would be entertaining clients and needed to appear successful. The employees saw the action for what it was: purely an ego stunt. The CEO never gained credibility, he was soon replaced, and the organization was again redesigned. It was an incredible waste of resources and human trust.

Individuals work together to do what they cannot do by themselves. In business, getting members of an organization to work together is often a challenge. Today's organizations are filled with creative, well-educated people. In complex and ever-changing environments, using the organization's collective intelligence is a better bet than relying on the wisdom of a few. Studies of flocking behavior in birds provide lessons about the nature of work and the use of collective resources. Engaging the total organization in the clutter campaign leverages flocking behavior. In some circles, wearing a Ralph Lauren Polo shirt is a sign of belonging to the "in crowd." It won't be long before being seen cleaning out a desk, updating a procedure, sweeping out the storage closet, or performing another tidy activity will have the same prestige.

ELIMINATING PERSONAL CLUTTER

Clean-up is a good time for self and individual assessment. It is a relaxed time during which to size each other up as team players and as individual contributors. Remember the volunteer clean-up projects or Habitat for Humanity building teams you participated in? They allowed a direct view of your team member's work ethic. Those who volunteer readily for these activities are usually the real team players. They are a bit more flexible and enjoy their work.

For most of us, clearing out organizational clutter also means clearing out personal clutter. When an employee is actively engaged in the job and has loyalty to the workplace, organization and personal space overlap. You can use this clutter campaign to clean out the cobwebs in your personal space and in your out-of-the-office life.

Figure 5.3 is similar to Figure 5.2. It focuses on a hierarchical structure. This time, however, it is an illustration of the leader's personal associations. A significant part of Executive Focus is individual. To be effective in the workplace, we must have our personal life aligned. The leader and the leader's significant other need a personal planning model just as the organization needs a business planning model. The steps are pretty much the same.

Feed your own soul and remember to love life. The arts, literature, music, and humanities serve to remind us of the joy of being alive and being expressive, creative, and hopeful. Hope keeps the engine running. Parents teach their children how to rhyme, sing, color, dance, and make music because those are all hopeful activities.

Use Figure 5.3 to guide you in reducing the clutter in your personal life and relationships. Be honest with yourself. If you do not like golf, do not play it. If it has been 30 years since you moved and the kids' teddy bears are still in the attic, invite those children to come for their stuff before you have that huge yard sale. Are you, like many of us, on way too many Boards? Which ones are "in name only" by now? Keep the ones that help you politically and in the community. Step away from the rest. Let someone else volunteer. How many magazines do you receive

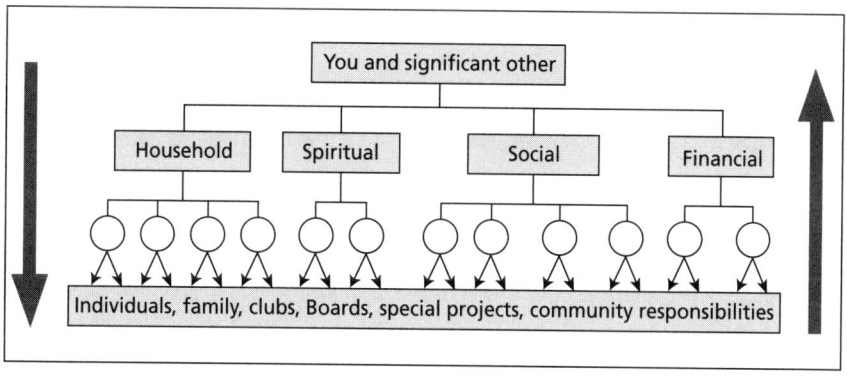

Figure 5.3 Personal clutter top down, bottom up.

every month? Are you still trying to keep up with all of them? Start weeding out the subscriptions. How many committees are you on at church? How many soccer games do you referee, even now that your children are no longer on the team? Are you still tracking all your own stocks? You get the idea. Lighten up your surroundings; it will lighten up your perspective.

SUMMING UP

Engage your employees and your family with mission, meaning, and cause. As the clean-up of Ground Zero and the Pentagon ended, we heard the words "under budget and ahead of schedule." How was this sad job done many months ahead of projections? One worker said: "The work may be the same, but the meaning is different." Every job has the value of making the world a better place by relieving pain, restoring hope, or adding beauty. Help your employees or family connect with the deepest values behind what they do, and you will have an inspired, energetic, mission-driven circle of friends and associates.

Next time you are stumped with a challenging business decision, take a walk instead of barging through the process. There is a strong relationship between physical activity and mental effectiveness. You may not be consciously thinking about the issues. You may simply be enjoying the walk when suddenly your subconscious comes up with a potential solution to what was bothering you. Relax; let go of the disruptions; focus on what is important.

Create a supportive environment. SRI CEO Curtis Carlson said: "Most people want to do a good job, and can achieve remarkable results if you create an environment that supports them. When you tap into that need, you find people who are incredibly resilient. They'll work incredible hours. They'll wake up in the morning thinking about their work. They'll suffer a hundred defeats because they see the opportunity to make a significant impact."

Having a good attitude is free. We cannot always choose the conditions under which we work, but we can always choose our attitude. Stephen Covey writes in *The 8th Habit*: "There is nothing as fast as the speed of trust. It's faster than anything you can think about. It's faster than the Internet. Trust is the glue of life. It is the glue that holds organizations, cultures, and relationships together. Ironically it comes from the speed of going slow. With people, fast is slow and slow is fast. Reflect on an employee who you completely trust with your biggest projects/tasks, and think of how much time it has taken to build up that trust. Develop a plan to build or rebuild a relationship of trust that does not exist now."

Sometimes going slow is preferable to speeding into the future. These days the Christmas season begins right after the 4th of July. Retailers start earlier and earlier every year. They are trying to rush us into the future and we let them do it every year. We must ask ourselves why we as a society are always running full-speed forward into the future and not enjoying the present. Focus on what really matters at the right time and the right place.

Reducing the clutter and getting down to what really matters is a labor of trust. We trust each other to know what has to be done. We trust ourselves to use what is left with integrity and responsibility. Enjoy your newly open workspace, living space, and personal space.

6
Organizational Momentum

- Do you ever worry about getting your plans executed?
- Do plans sometimes just fade off into the sunset without results?
- Do you wrestle with the choice of whom to assign to what projects?
- Do you have dead wood in the organization that should be trimmed?

If you answered "yes" to these questions, then this chapter will help you achieve the results you have planned for so diligently. As leaders, our responsibility is to get things done through others. Once a company leaves the entrepreneurial stage, we cannot do it all ourselves. As leaders, we must create a motivating environment in which others help lead the wagon train where it needs to go.

Once you decide where to take the organization, how do you line up the wagons and get the train moving? What are the things that make your organization move forward?

Chapter 4 talked about different directions we can take the organization. Should we improve existing processes? Is a breakthrough redesign in order? Did the previous senior executive make radical changes and the Board now needs a caretaker leadership approach? Is it time to either grow or scale back the company? Each of these directions requires a specific design. None of them can effectively be realized without strong communication on your part and the total involvement of your direct reports and major stakeholders.

What data did you use to decide what direction to lead the company? If that data made sense to you, chances are your leadership team will agree with you if you share it. If you do not get consensus from your team, find out why. Either you are making too big a jump for them to follow, or there are other circumstances you have not yet uncovered that may further influence your decision.

One definition of leadership is the ability to take others someplace we would not go ourselves. Establishing the kinetic energy required to move a complex organization is not a simple task. Find out what matters most to those who will help you move the organization and use those values and results to build the kinetic energy forward. Use your Dark Energy to light a fire under your team.

Many of us in senior leadership are well along in our lives, with grown families. We want to make a difference and do great things. It is possible, however, that when we step back, we see that we have been in a bit of a rut, running between e-mail and meetings all day. There's a realization that we only have so much time left, and that if we want to accomplish something, we have to move. Use this unrealized achievement need to generate excitement for your vision of the future. Get to know each of your senior leaders. Find out what makes them tick. There may be one or two who are "retired in grade" and who should be humanely moved to the sidelines before you can truly flip the "GO" switch. Chapter 2, Homeland and Personal Security, discusses the characteristics of these individuals. Now is the time to either change their minds or move them out.

A good thing about the new generation is that they do not feel hindered by a lack of experience before seeking promotion into leadership positions. They no longer feel the need to earn a position through long years of proving themselves. Generation X workers expect to be given advanced responsibility when they are ready for it, not when a slot opens because someone who was there before them got a chance. The challenge with Generation X workers is to get them involved at the level they desire before they become impatient and take their talents elsewhere.

Much is written in current business literature about succession planning. Use this information to involve the seasoned leadership as well as the ladder-climbing newer generation in building your long-term organization. The existing senior management will be part of the discovery process that identifies required characteristics for your leadership team. There is something cathartic about writing our own epitaph. It is a lot easier to accept stepping down when it was "our idea" rather than having it forced upon us by someone else. Get to know the existing senior management team well enough to know who to keep and who to guide toward another phase in their career.

Working with the new generation of leaders may be a mixed experience. On the one hand, it is exhilarating to work with all that energy. Their filtering system for assessing situations and information is still fresh. There is less of what the authors call "scar tissue" to obscure their ability to view positive outcomes for the future of the organization. On the other hand, there is a tremendous impatience for results. The wildly interruption-driven learning style of the video-game generation has little experience with long-term planning, iterative organizational redesign, and the recognition of others who have earned a seat at the table before they do. Keeping these young warriors engaged and committed to the future success of the company may be a challenge.

Orchestrate an active involvement strategy for all those you want as part of your long-term leadership team. Use the seasoned executives in a coaching role. Ask them to identify and preserve those parts of the corporate culture that are useful transitions for where you need to be in the future. Provide them with the opportunity to fashion a productive spot within the new organization. Likewise, involve the newer leaders in building their own succession plan. Ask them to establish realistic timelines and general contribution opportunities that are consistent with the direction you need to take the organization. Work with them to balance the needs of the organization for effective growth and their own need for recognition and career attainment. Be honest with them about how much advancement is possible in what amount of time. Rarely are we able to promote the younger leaders as quickly as they desire. Involving them in the logic of organizational design may help establish more reasonable expectations.

Remember your own needs as you work with the needs of the leadership team. Executive Focus is about using your talents to get where you want to be. The organization is a vehicle for your own progression. Include your personal vision in the success-planning you establish. You may or may not wish to share all of your personal plans with everyone. They are concerned with their own futures.

WHAT MOMENTUM DO YOU CREATE?

All momentum is not created equal. Chapter 4 introduces four different directions for you to take as the incoming senior executive:

1. Clean up/reorganize
2. Maintain
3. Grow
4. Downsize

Clean up/reorganize is the easiest. There are many models available for organizational assessment, visioning, gap analysis, and process improvement. Find the one that fits your company culture and use it.

Maintenance, as mentioned in Chapter 4, may seem to be the easiest. In actuality, it may be the most difficult for you as a new leader to get your spirit around. If the organization is quiet, why is that a good thing? What causes your Board of Directors to choose a status quo strategy? What challenges are there in this strategy for you to sink your teeth into as a growing leader? How do you motivate a leadership team to feel fulfilled by excellent deployment of a maintenance strategy? The authors have found it useful to design a modified growth or reorganization strategy as a loosely veiled maintenance gig. That way, when you give your semi-annual report to the stockholders, you have some great upward moving trend charts to show for your efforts.

The growth strategy is the rollercoaster ride all of us dream of in business school. This is the easy road for generating forward energy within the whole organization. Identify the vision, set the goals, develop the strategy, wave the flag, and sound the charge. Rally the troops around a good organizational design and step aside so the tacticians can make it happen. Your job as the senior leader is to be cheerleader, customer relationship manager, and show-horse for the media.

Downsizing is another matter. This is the one that hurts. No one likes to admit we bit off more than we can chew. Success comes from admitting it, designing a better organization, and seeing it through to a minimally painful conclusion. The good part of this message is that when we are successful in leading a complex organization into a more compact configuration, we are in great demand with other organizations who know they must travel the same pathway.

WHAT DID I DO TO REACH THIS STATE?

External drivers for organizational change can be viewed from three perspectives: capital markets, customer and product markets, and geopolitical environments. Chapter 2, Homeland and Personal Security, reviewed the Balanced Scorecard components that help us gather and interpret the leading and lagging indicators that support our decisions for organizational direction. Our role as leader is one of systematically presenting a macroeconomic view of our competitive environment so major stakeholders have a clear sense of how various economic and sociopolitical factors affect the business.

Our executive challenge centers on strategy formation and implementation. Focusing on competitive positioning helps the company to understand how to orient the business in increasingly dynamic markets and provides strategies to recognize and respond to threats in the marketplace. Get your direct reports focused on the organizational, systems, and people parts of the equation. As a leader, what must you do to cause the organization to change? The change imperative will differ depending on how the organization arrived at the position in which you now find yourself.

Reorganization, maintenance, growth, and downsizing require different strategies for successful implementation. The implication is that you must put the resources in place to meet and exceed the expectations of your primary customer while you look after your other constituents on an as-needed basis.

To what extent are people in the organization committed to helping others achieve shared goals? In some situations—a Wall Street trading floor or a car dealership, for example—people are paid on commission; it doesn't matter if they're committed to helping others. In other organizations, commitment to the whole is enormously important.

Recent research in effective business leadership focuses on creative tension. We ask how managers can create tension in the business to promote or stimulate innovation across internal units. We illustrate mechanisms that will encourage dialogue across internal boundaries and look at techniques such as stretch goals to get people to think outside the box.

The measures discussed in Chapter 2, when developed specifically in support of the most important goals of the organization, can create this business tension. If we know that something we do makes the needle quiver on one of our indicators, we are more likely to either repeat that effort or stop doing it, depending on which way the indicator moved. We are learning creatures. We do what is reinforced. Establish what is important to your customers, internal and external, and work with employees at all levels of the organization to identify measures that tell you when you are meeting or exceeding those requirements. Track the measures and report them on a consistent and scheduled basis. When you hit the target on those measures, look for the next set of unmet requirements while maintaining your performance on the original set.

You need not do this alone. Involving others in this march toward greatness is a team effort. You need strategic, tactical, and operational measures to move the organization. Assign responsibility and accountability to people at those three levels of leadership. Stay in touch with them, listen to them, share your ideas and decisions with them, and celebrate when they hand you the results you planned. When the results do not come in, do not kill the messenger. Include them in the problem solving, make the adjustments, and try again.

Encourage your employees to come to their next level of management with observations, issues, concerns, problems, and potential solutions. You may want to share that it's not wise to come back with a know-it-all attitude. They are not ready to save the company simply because the CEO has empowered them and shown faith in their abilities. On the other hand, do expect them to return with some substantive ideas about how to create significant movement toward corporate goals.

You are the ultimate coach for the organization. Effective coaching may be the single most important skill you can learn. Coaching is the art of drawing forth potential onto the canvas of value creation. Use the language of coaching—questions—to build awareness, build commitment, and build practice. Instead of being simply an executive order-giver, move to being a leader-coach by practicing the art of listening and asking questions. In doing so, you will help the organization find its way through challenges and problems. Leading through provocative, reflective questions will engage people and their potential more powerfully than being the expert problem-solver. Such coaching awakens possibilities. People who are excited about possibilities have the energy to move forward. They have momentum.

KINETIC ENERGY AND DARK ENERGY

Once you get the folks moving, how do you keep them moving? One of the authors remembers a performer who spun plates on sticks on the Ed Sullivan show of the 1950s. The idea was to start as many plates spinning as possible and then move up and down the line, providing each stick with just enough energy to keep the plate balanced and spinning on top. Keeping the organization going is much like keeping the plates spinning. Once the plates are moving, they have kinetic energy. It takes less effort to maintain the momentum than it does to get it started.

As the executive, you and your strategic planning committee identify the plates that should be spinning. Your leadership team takes over to put the plans in place and drill the tactics and operations down into the many layers of the organization. An effective reward and recognition program is an integral part of the momentum process. Since you can't make your team or organization into something that you are not, it must start with you. What motivates you to seek out new opportunities? What generates your Dark Energy? What keeps you excited about where you are going and, subsequently, where the organization is going?

REWARD WHAT YOU WANT TO CONTINUE

Whose needs are your recognition and reward systems designed to serve? What are the goals? Are they to manipulate, control, and "motivate"? Or do they build an atmosphere of helpfulness, appreciation, and high energy? How do you know? As with beauty, quality, and customer service, reward and recognition are in the eye of the beholder. Plan your recognition system to tie closely with your measurement and monitoring system. You probably like being recognized for doing things that are important. Your employees feel the same way.

Work with your leadership team to blend customer and partner input with your organization's vision, values, purpose, strategic imperatives, and improvement goals. Set up systems, programs, and training and provide a personal leadership example that gets customers and partners involved in giving frequent recognition and appreciation to each other. Be clear about what is to be rewarded and recognized and by whom. Move management out of the role of deciding who gets rewarded and recognized for what behaviors. Keep measurements, improvement progress, and recognition highly visible.

Use scoreboards, bulletin boards, voice mail, electronic or printed announcements, and the like. Momentum comes from seeing a direct relationship between action and reaction. "The goal is this; we met or exceeded the goal; therefore *this* happens."

Reward and recognition are not difficult and you'll be surprised at just how easy it is to raise the performance bar in your organization.

EMPLOY ORGANIZATIONAL AND PERSONAL MOMENTUM

Develop the habit of pointing out the positive at home, with friends, with neighbors, at social activities, and so on. Sincere recognition skills and genuine appreciation habits aren't turned on at work and turned off when you go home (flattery and manipulation can be). Your Executive Focus is tied not only to your work environment, but to the whole you. Momentum is not just an office phenomenon. It is important for your family and community goals, too.

Make sure there's a good balance between measuring, tracking, and rewarding current performance and improvement. People who do well today but aren't improving won't help your organization get better. Momentum is not maintenance. Momentum is forward motion that exhibits energy.

Anyone who's not continually improving will eventually become a liability. The plates must keep spinning on the sticks. Even better, we must figure out how to add more sticks and more plates. That is where teamwork comes in. One person can spin a few plates. Many people working together can spin a lot of plates.

Recognition and excitement about meeting goals comes from involving people in getting things done. Build important jobs around the right people. Align good people with what they like to do and what needs doing. Helping people to grow, expand, and move to new challenges and opportunities is one of the best ways to show genuine appreciation for their efforts. Owning a piece of our own forward motion is a tremendous energy creator. Use this ownership to support your organizational momentum.

7
Job and Place Mismatch

- Are you unhappy in your current job?
- Do you feel your skills and current job responsibilities are not in sync?
- Are you ready to go but not sure where to go?
- Do you want to re-orient yourself but not sure what direction to take?

If you answered "yes" to these questions, then you are experiencing the job-and-place mismatch phenomenon. Part of your Executive Focus strategy is to develop a game plan to find the right alignment between your skills, education, experience, knowledge, and proficiency and the job you have or want to have in the near future.

SOUND ADVICE

Some sound advice one of the authors received from his first boss was, "The day you get a new job is the time to start looking for the next one." Career planning never stops. It is something you must always keep in the forefront of your mind. You must never let it slip out of sight lest it be too late when you eventually try to revive it. The intensity with which you look for a new job will vary over time, but the idea is to start planning your next career move immediately upon beginning your latest job. Keep a constant focus on opportunities that lie beyond your current position. If you wait too long you may find yourself pushed into the "job-finding panic" mode. Things change quickly in the world of work. Do not let unexpected change have an adverse impact on your career plans. This is pro-active career advice. Heed it and let it serve you well for a long time.

The "job" is the what, skills are the how, and focus is the goals to be accomplished, both personal and professional. The job is the vehicle that allows you to demonstrate your skills and ability in the marketplace. The job is the experience part of the career equation; it gives you visibility in the marketplace and a chance to be seen by others. The job allows you to showcase yourself in either a positive or negative light that shines strongly or weakly depending upon your performance.

The other part of the career equation is the "place," where you are in your Executive Growth life span. It is an indicator of how you have grown over the years. When combined successfully with the job, we get the perfect match: the right job at the right place in your life.

Think about the following four scenarios concerning the job-and-place mismatch phenomenon, shown in Figure 7.1:

1. The Right Job at the Right Place In Your Life

This happens because of good career planning. The job needs are a perfect match to where you are in your life. Your skills, education, experience, knowledge, and proficiency are all in the right place in your life and are exactly what is needed to do the job successfully. This is a perfect match and your Executive Focus is at its maximum efficiency.

2. The Wrong Job at the Right Place In Your Life

Too often this happens when you are not able to move to a new position and your skills, education, experience, knowledge, and proficiency have all evolved beyond the needs of the job you currently hold. This leads to feelings of uneasiness and unhappiness. This mismatch will cause problems at work. You will start losing your Executive Focus and start feeling that

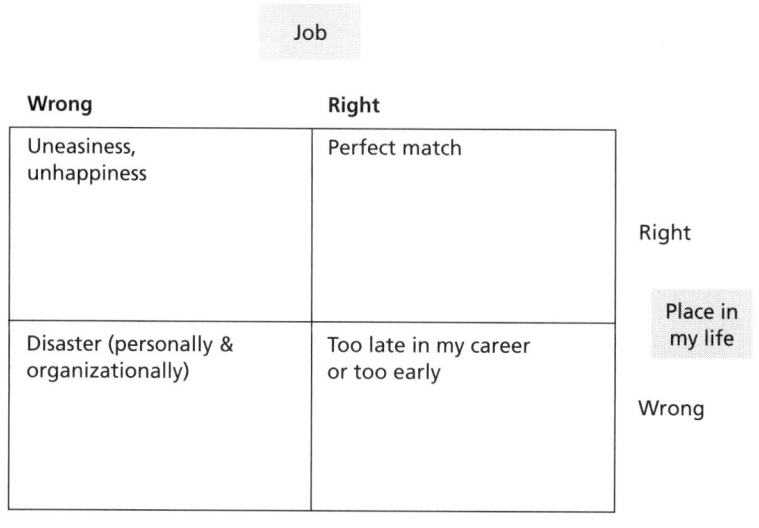

Figure 7.1 Job-and-place mismatch phenomenon.

you do not want to go to work each day. If this state is allowed to exist, over time it will lead to job performance problems and job dissatisfaction.

This happens when you lose sight of what you want to achieve in your career and become bogged down in the day-to-day drudgeries of everyday work and life. You must take time each day or each week to focus on what you want to achieve in your career and make sure you are on track to achieve your goals. You want to keep your career objectives on track and constantly focus on positioning yourself to make that happen. You can schedule things to happen if you are willing to invest the time and energy into your career.

3. The Right Job at the Wrong Place In Your Life

This happens either too early or too late in your career. Your skills, education, experience, knowledge, and proficiency are deficient in regards to the job you currently have or have been offered. You may have an opportunity to move quickly into a job that is above your head but one to which you will aspire in a couple of years. The personal cost of trying to make a situation like this work is very high. You may have to sacrifice your personal life in order to build skills, education, experience, knowledge, and proficiency very quickly in order to succeed. There is only so much time in a day. Sacrificing your personal life for career gain is always an option, but one that may have long-term negative consequences for you and your family.

You can remedy this by quickly pushing your skills, education, experience, knowledge, and proficiency to the level required to do your job. This is difficult but doable if you apply yourself to the task. At this point you must understand whether it is knowledge or proficiency you lack. We all try to be proficient, but we may need only to be knowledgeable to do the task at hand.

4. The Wrong Job at the Wrong Place In Your Life

This is a disaster for you and the organization. Your skills, education, experience, knowledge, and proficiency are 180 degrees out of alignment with the job's needs. Sometimes this happens when you get a new job and realize very quickly that it is not what you wanted or expected it to be. Sometimes the best you get out of a situation like this is a deep battle scar; the worst could be a humiliating failure that follows you for years as you try to rebuild your career.

Throughout an executive's career there are a few times where you have the right job at the right time in your life. When the right job and the right place perfectly match up, everything is in alignment with your skills, your desires, and the organization's needs. This is usually a happy time in your life. Having this alignment at work spills over into your personal life and makes interactions with your family and friends a positive experience at the same time.

Unfortunately, this is not a static state that remains in alignment forever. It is always being impacted by four forces that can throw a perfect state totally out of alignment and into a transition zone. The four forces acting against you, shown in Figure 7.2, are:

1. *Time*—never stands still and always brings new changes into your life over which you have no control.

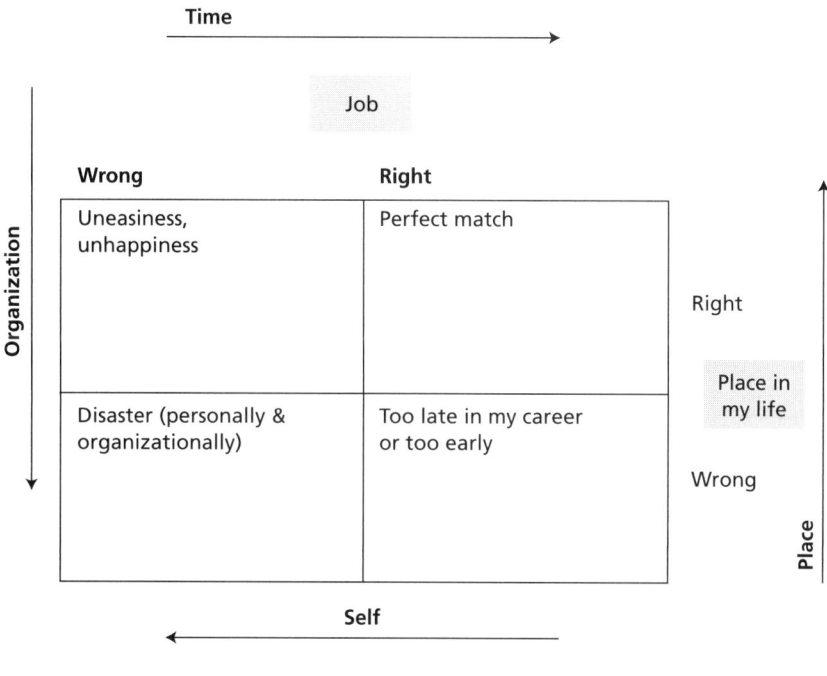

Figure 7.2 Forces affecting career alignment.

2. *Place*—changes in your skills, education, knowledge, proficiency, wants, needs, and desires.
3. *Organization*—evolves and changes as people come and go, and brings a new culture to the organization that may not be in alignment with your wants, needs, and desires.
4. *Self*—you constantly grow and change in relation to your surroundings, and your changed wants and needs may not be satisfied in your current situation.

These four forces are not static but act with different intensity at different times to force you out of a comfort zone and into a transition zone. As soon as you respond to the most powerful one, the next one begins to force you into a new transition zone. These forces are in constant motion.

Transition zones appear suddenly and with different intensities. Something might happen at the office, such as the sudden departure of a senior executive for whom you work, perhaps because of death or scandal. The replacement may want to change everything you have been involved with developing. It could be that a competitor catches your company off guard by introducing a new product and you rapidly lose market share. Your company could be sold or taken over, with an immediate force reduction at your level. You go part time to graduate school to earn an advanced degree, only to find that your current job feels confining and that you cannot use your new skills. You could receive a large inheritance that would change your wants and desires both professionally and personally.

The ability and the time required to recognize, react, and reorient yourself out of a transition zone depends on where you are in your career path. Early on in your career, when you were first out of college, there were many employment opportunities, careers, and escape paths to get you out of a transition zone and back on track. As you mature and narrow the focus of your executive career, opportunities to escape from a transition zone are fewer. You may be stuck in this zone for a while. Life in a transition zone can be unpleasant because it is filled with uncertainty, which can lead to feelings of stress.

When you recognize that you have moved into a transition zone you must immediately begin to develop an action plan that will take you back to the right job and right place. During this time in the transition zone things can become unsettling both in your work and in your personal life. New pressures that were not there a few weeks ago appear and must be dealt with so as to keep you focused on executing your action plan.

Transition zones are uncomfortable because they are undefined, full of uncertainty, and without rules or guidelines that will help you escape. What worked the last time may not work this time. It is difficult to gauge the size and shape of a transition zone when you enter it. At first it may look like a black hole that is sucking you down into a sense of despair.

Over the years the authors have identified early warning signals that will alert you to the start of a transition zone:

- **Uneasiness:** You feel a sense of uneasiness at the next level above you. Your boss may be sending out mixed signals about how well the organization is doing. Your boss may be cancelling meetings with you and your co-workers. When the boss does meet with you there is a feeling of awkwardness. Rumors may be circulating about the company's current performance. Executives at your level have recently resigned and replacements are not being sought. A key project or client has been lost.

  A transition zone may have begun. You must quickly assess how far into the zone you have ventured and what decisions must be made to keep your Executive Focus and career on track.

- **Unhappiness:** Something has changed or is changing in your life and it is making you anxious. You cannot put your finger on it, but something is bugging you either at work or in your personal life and you want to make a change. You are not sure what that change is at the moment, but something is changing in you as a person.

  There may be a transition zone on the near horizon and you must take time to figure out what is going on in your life. You can control this type of transition zone by carefully analyzing what is going on with you as a person. First determine what is driving you to want change; then decide how to make the change. This type of transition zone change is easy to manage because you can control it in private. No one need know what you did to change. It is unlike the zone changes where you are in them with others in a very public arena.

- **Un-seasonableness:** Like the weather, organizations go through seasons and phases. There are profit seasons, improvement seasons, re-organization seasons, change seasons, and so on. After a while we become accustomed to these changing seasons and we can predict them with some certainty. When we see the boss reading a book on the latest management fad, we can almost predict that within a few weeks everyone will be reading the book. Eventually the boss will start pushing everyone to implement the ideas; a few months later it will have died a natural death and you can await the next fad.

You may start to see a change in seasons *not* suited to the current condition: consultants who appear without warning to analyze aspects of your work area; "we went from a 30% profit last quarter to a 30% loss this quarter;" clients defecting to the competition in droves; and so on. There may be a transition zone on the near horizon.

- **Un-willingness:** You begin to notice a change in the organization's willingness to tackle tough issues or problems. In the past, the organization had the collective will to make necessary changes to keep itself on the right track. If there was a budget problem or staffing issue, the organization as a collective whole pulled together to make things right. Now you notice that everyone has gone into a protective mode and that finger pointing and blame are the order of the day. This may signal that the organization is in, or is going into, a transition zone that may drag you into to it as well.

HOW TO HANDLE REPEATED TRIPS TO THE TRANSITION ZONE

First, realize that everything is changing constantly and that nothing lasts forever. Once you find the perfect place, it begins to change and continues to change until you are no longer in alignment. You may not like the fact that things are changing and forcing you out of your comfort zone. Common reactions to change are denial and anger, but the fact remains that *things do change* and *you cannot control the change.* Both of these reactions are time wasters; you will stress yourself and waste valuable time you could be using to find a better position that will re-establish your comfort zone. Accept that life is constant change and move on in a manner that is least disruptive to you and your career.

Second, focus on the fact that you must grow and expand. You must constantly expand your proficiency and knowledge of your business, and understand how what is happening around you in the outside world will affect you. Monitor what your colleagues are doing to increase their Dark Energy and expand their universe. If you don't let warning signs pass you by, you won't find yourself saying "If I had only…," or "I could have…," or "I should have…."

Third, maintain a positive "can do" attitude and be realistic with yourself and your abilities. The day may come when you have to admit to yourself that "this is as good as it gets." Recognize that this may be the threshold from which you can rise no further, and make yourself happy and productive.

As we pointed out in Chapter 4, you must keep yourself attuned to what you are sensing, feeling, and seeing on a daily basis, and be constantly alert to changes that may force you out of your comfort zone and into a transition zone. You must be forward-planning all the time, with Plan A, Plan B, and Plan C ready to go when it's necessary to exit a transition zone. This is the essence of career planning. This is "The day you get a new job is the time to start looking for a next one" Executive Focus' focus.

Transition zones are not a bad thing but rather an opportunity that forces you to move on to a new and better place, one that is aligned with your desires, skills, education, knowledge, and proficiency…the right place in your career.

8
Achievement and Avoidance Goals

- Are you ready to go but not sure where to go?
- Do you have limited direction in your career?
- Do you feel lost in the workplace?
- Are you ready to re-orient yourself but not sure what direction to take?

If you answered "yes" to these questions, then you have probably not set any meaningful life and career goals. Goal setting is a key ingredient to developing a life and career plan that will bring you satisfaction and fulfillment. Part of your Executive Focus strategy is to develop a game plan in order to find the right alignment between your skills, education, experience, knowledge, and proficiency and the job you have or want to have in the near future. In order to do this, you must set goals so you can measure your progress and know whether you are on track or need to adjust your Executive Focus strategy.

Goal setting is a process of introspection that leads to understanding what in your work life will make you feel satisfied and self-fulfilled. When we have meaningful goals that are achieved on a regular basis we tend to be fully engaged in our work and our life is in balance. Often we tend to focus on goals that must be achieved and we lose site of goals for situations we must avoid. Avoidance goals are just as important as achievement goals to our Executive Focus strategy because they help us determine those things we want to avoid in the future. Avoidance goals help us to avoid jumping out of the frying pan and into the fire. Avoidance goals could be viewed as a means to reduce the risk of career change that does not benefit us in the long run. If we ignore avoidance goals in our career and life planning, we wind up with nothing more than an escape plan, which may lead into a situation worse than the one we just left.

At some point we all had a course in statistics and studied hypothesis testing. In hypothesis testing we learned that there is a struggle between two types of errors found in a sampling plan. The Type I error causes us to reject something we should have accepted. The Type II error causes us to accept something we should have rejected. We can reduce the risk of one type of error at the expense of increasing the risk of the other. We learned that we could never be free of both errors but that we could reduce the risk of both by increasing our sample size. Increasing the sample size is costly and takes time, particularly if we want to make a quick decision. As decision makers we must decide which error is the most serious to our decision-making process and then develop a sampling strategy.

What you want from your next career move is somewhat dependent on your age and where you are now. A younger worker may want position, money, title, and fast advancement. Once you hit middle age, you may be in your peak earning years and want things such as a flexible work schedule, better benefits, and more vacation time. Salary may be secondary to other concerns. Those closer to retirement age may be more interested in continuity of health benefits and generous retirement plans. The ability to work part-time to keep active after retirement may be of top concern.

In this book our focus has been on career and life planning to achieve a balance in life and work and on setting career achievement goals. If accomplished, these would lead us to the state we are seeking. Achievement goals could be viewed as a way to reduce the Type I error of rejecting a career move that would benefit our future state. Achievement goals must be developed very carefully so they fully reflect what we really want to achieve in our next career move.

Achievement goals keep us focused on the end point. The measurement of achievement goals is important because it lets us know where we are at any point in time in the attainment of specific goals.

When developing achievement and avoidance goals we must focus on the vital few and not the trivial many. Goal development takes time and requires the prioritization of our many wants and needs into the vital few that we *must* attain. In order to be measurable and trackable, goals must be specific and concisely written. Concise and specific goals help us communicate clearly to prospective employers exactly what we want in a job they may wish to see us fill.

Some categories and examples of Achievement Goals are:

- *Pay and Benefits:*
  - Increased pay
  - Better benefits
  - Flexibility in work hours and location
  - Continuity of benefits in retirement
  - Retirement and 401(k) plans

  The Pay and Benefit category is often developed first when we start a career and life plan because it affects us every time we pay a bill or schedule a health appointment. We are confronted daily by the quality or lack of quality in the pay and benefits package of our current employer and we want more. In today's environment of cafeteria benefit plans and bonus promises instead of pay raises, we may feel as though we are on the short end of the stick. We must carefully develop realistic achievement goals for this category given the market environment in which we find ourselves selling our talents.

- *Work:*
  - Interesting and varied
  - Challenging assignments
  - Engaging
  - Motivating
  - Non-routine
  - Within our control
  - Worthy of pride and respect

  As we develop career and life plan achievement goals, we often discover that the work category stirs us the most. It becomes more important than pay and benefits because the work itself is what motivates us to get up in the morning with a positive attitude. Interesting, varied, and challenging work makes an engaged and motivated employee. Work that motivates us provides a feeling of accomplishment and pride. Interesting, varied, and challenging work gives us an opportunity to show off our skills and talent to upper management. Every job involves some routine, but we want a realistic balance between routine work and challenging and engaging assignments.

- *Advancement:*
  - More authority
  - Increased managerial responsibility
  - Better utilization of skills and experience
  - Promotion from within

  Achieving the goals we set in the work category will help set the stage for the career advancement we desire in the future. If we are able to perform and successfully complete interesting, varied, and challenging work assignments, we will be noticed by upper management and move up the management ladder.

- *Employer:*
  - Balanced work and life
  - Improved self-esteem
  - Pride
  - Career development opportunities

  We all want to work for a company where other people want to work, one for which we're motivated to check for job openings on a regular basis. Having pride in an employer and what the company does for its people and for the economy is a strong motivator. Good employers are involved with their employees' well being and career development. They provide an environment that promotes a healthy balance between work and life. If employers are interested in their employees and the employees are proud of the company, a strong cycle of reinforcement leads to happy employees and higher productivity.

When we find an organization we would like to pursue, we should remember the concept of Avoidance Goals. A checklist of things we want to avoid in the next career move can be helpful. These become our personal Avoidance Goals. A list of avoidance goals can help reduce the risk of a classic Type II error, accepting a career change that would not benefit us in the long run. If we ignore avoidance goals in career and life planning, we wind up with nothing more than an escape plan, which may lead into a situation that is worse than the one we just left.

An escape plan may be nothing more than simply running after the first thing that looks better than our current situation. An escape plan is no plan at all if we just jump at the first thing that looks better on the surface. We need to explore below the surface in order to fully understand what we might be getting ourselves into in a new situation. Remember, the devil you know is sometimes better than the one you do not.

The following are some examples of Avoidance Goals.

- *Management:*
  - Micro managers
  - An overbearing boss
  - Crisis mode as a way of life
  - A constant do-more-with-less philosophy
  - Meetings mania

  We have all seen office sitcoms and movies featuring a bad boss in an organization where we would not want to work. You may have worked for one of these, the overbearing, toxic boss who functions as a dictator and imposes his will on everyone and everything that is done in the office. At some point you may have worked for the micro manager who never lets anybody do anything without her approval. If you put these two types together and add to them an organization in continuous crisis mode where meetings replace action, you have a work situation that is a disaster for the employees. When you contemplate a life and career move, you must ask yourself if the motivation is the management or the company. If the motivation is your current management, reflect this in your life and career plan. You may want to focus your search inside your current company because you have a vested interest in staying.

- *Work Environment:*
  - No career development opportunities
  - Overbearing co-workers
  - Lack of respect
  - Life in a cubicle corral
  - Whining co-workers
  - Constant fear of layoff
  - Chronic understaffing

  A pleasant work environment is an important ingredient for developing motivation at work.

Employees who feel trapped in a dead-end job with no advancement opportunity tend to become detached from the organization and eventually leave. An environment of fear, that this Friday will be the layoff, is toxic. The physical work environment is important to making employees productive. Life in a cubicle corral can be a demotivator for workers crowded into a small, noisy work space. People must feel respected and they need privacy and quiet in order to conduct the work they have been assigned. As you consider a change in position, it is important to look at where the potential employer expects you will work.

- *Advancement:*
  - Underutilized skills and experience
  - Exclusion from the mainstream
  - Lack of training opportunities
  - A sense of being boxed in

When interviewing for a new position you must thoroughly investigate these important areas. One of the main reasons people move to new employers is to better their skills and enlarge their experience. If you wind up with a position that does not let you expand your horizons, you will begin to fall behind your peers. When accepting a new position it is reasonable and important to ask for guarantees that you will have an opportunity to develop yourself professionally. When you are exploring a new position, remember to "trust but verify." Trust what they promise you but verify it as you meet the people you may be working with in the future.

- *Co-workers:*
  - Impose on my space
  - Hold loud conversations
  - Shirk assignments and push work on to others
  - Talk and behave crudely
  - Play loud music

- Try to involve me in their personal dramas
- Abuse my personal belongings

Being surrounded by co-workers who whine constantly about job conditions and the organization tends to damage a person's motivation. This category of avoidance goals is really about your co-workers manners, or lack of manners. Cubicle protocol is an important part of the work environment; it sets the tone for how others respect you and each other. While you are interviewing, spend some time in the area where you will work, if possible. Within fifteen minutes you will have insight into how people operate there. Those few minutes will give you a sense of both the noise level and the level of respect those workers show each other. Watch for interruptions while interviewing with a potential co-worker or teammate. If someone walks right in and interrupts without warning, the danger flags should go up.

- *Personal:*
  - Lowered self-esteem
  - Overworked
  - Unappreciated
  - Assigned to dead-end or ineffectual teams
  - Locked into current job because company will not replace my skills
  - Long commute
  - Traffic

Personal avoidance goals vary from one individual to another, but they almost always revolve around issues that are a source of irritation in your current position. Long commutes, too much work, too little appreciation, and dead-end assignments are common things people want to avoid in the next position. People have different levels of tolerance for what they will put up with in a situation. What bothers one person may not bother another. The category of personal avoidance goals is one that will vary by individual and thus is difficult to generalize. You may not achieve all of your personal avoidance goals, but you can strive to reach as many as possible.

Achievement and avoidance goal setting are important parts of establishing a life and career plan. Goals help guide us and keep us on track. Goals are not static but must be updated as circumstances evolve over time. A measurement system will let us know when goals must be updated. Measurement of goals keeps us grounded and focused on where we are in the process of achieving our life and career plan. Measurement may tell us what we want to hear (that we are on track), or it may tell us we have lost our way, that we are off track and not achieving what we want. Whatever measurement system we set up to monitor achievement and avoidance goals, it must have the following characteristics:

- *Simple to compute.* We want to easily collect data that will allow us to monitor our achievement and avoidance goals. If the data are easily collected, it will motivate us to do it on a regular basis. The data we collect may be quantitative or qualitative. We can track pay and benefits quantitatively while measuring enjoyment of work on a qualitative scale.

- *Done on a regular basis.* To be meaningful, measurement must be done on a regular basis so we can observe patterns and trends. Pay and benefits may be evaluated once a year when they are adjusted for the organization. Work enjoyment can be evaluated on a daily basis. The frequency of the measurement will be dictated by the type of achievement and avoidance goals we set and choose to monitor.

- *Early warning system.* The measurement system should provide us with data that we believe in and should clearly indicate when we have drifted off course and entered into the start of a transition zone. The ability to detect a transition zone will help us to move quickly to put life and career plan back on track.

- *Actionable.* When it's time to take action to correct a deviation in one or more of our achievement and avoidance goals, we must know how large the gap is. If the deviation is small, we may want to wait until the next measurement cycle to see whether it self-corrects. Large deviations require us to develop an action plan. It may take weeks or months to get back on track. A good measurement system will alert us early on and prevent the surprise of a large deviation. Once we know we are drifting we can make minor alterations to get back on track. Minor alterations are preferable to large course corrections because they are easier to accomplish.

It's important to take time and care in setting achievement and avoidance goals because they are the indicators that a life and career plan is being achieved. To make sure we are achieving our goals, we must track progress through a well-defined measurement system and quickly catch trends that show we are drifting off course. If we wait until we are really off course, recovery may take a long time. Recognizing when we are entering a transition zone allows us to gear up and refocus, to assure that we have the right job at the right place in life.

Having the right job at the right place in life happens because of good career planning. The job needs are a perfect match to where you are in life. Your skills, education, experience, knowledge, and proficiency are exactly what are needed to do the job successfully. As we mentioned in the previous chapter, this is a Perfect Match and your Executive Focus is at its maximum efficiency.

Remember, balancing life and career requires goals. You cannot score unless you make a goal. You need a goal to know when you have scored.

9
Sensory Indicators

- Do you feel overwhelmed with information?
- Do you feel paralyzed, unable to take action?
- Do you feel you are being shielded from bad news by your direct reports?
- Do you feel you are constantly being pushed to go faster and faster?

If you answered "yes" to these questions, then you must develop an early warning system that will alert you to changes taking place in your organization. Formal measurement systems can be precise but they are not always instantly available. In this chapter we discuss the development of sensory indicators to augment your formal measurement system and help you monitor your organization.

MEASUREMENT IS STRENGTH

We have all heard the saying that there is organizational strength in a measurement system that generates good numbers upon which to make sound decisions. We have all built dashboards to monitor how the organization is performing on key management indicators. Unfortunately, not everything can be measured quantitatively and precisely. Some of the best indicators of organization performance and future performance come from our senses. Although these sensory measurements are qualitative, they can be very accurate in determining current and future trends in the organization's ability to perform its designated mission and to satisfy our focus goals.

Sensory indicators have been around for a long time. One of our grandmothers used to say that she could feel in her bones when bad news was coming. When trying to keep your focus on track, you will need sensory indicators to help you evaluate your progress. They will alert you if you or your organization is beginning to slip, or if you are being pushed into a transition zone that will require your attention.

The authors have found four focus sensory indicators that must be monitored on a regular basis, as shown in Figure 9.1. They are:

- Seeing
- Hearing
- Feeling
- Sensing

These four sensory indicators can give you a pretty accurate pulse of the organization's state of health. These sensory indicators must be monitored on a regular basis so you always have an ongoing organizational analysis process monitoring and measuring what action must be taken.

- *What Am I Seeing?* This is the first item for consideration in Figure 9.1. When you walk around the organization on your sensory tours, start by observing how the organization looks physically. A cluttered, deteriorating, dirty, or unkempt appearance is an indicator of how employees are maintaining and respecting the place where they work. This is also an indication of how current management is permitting the organization to deteriorate, which usually spills over to the way employees and customers are treated. If the company

What am I seeing?	What am I hearing?	What am I feeling?	What am I sensing?	What does it mean?	What action should I take?

Figure 9.1 Sensory indicators for ongoing organizational analysis.

is not investing in its facilities, ask yourself where else are they not investing. What are the long-term consequences of these actions?

On your walking tour look at how offices are kept and at the condition of the bathrooms and stairwells. If they are dirty, realize that these are not the only places that should be cleaned. How people treat the workplace, the place where they live for many hours a day, is an indicator of the respect they have for the organization.

Refer to Chapter 5, Personal and Organizational Clutter. The concept of "noise" is not just for statistical process control. Noise in an organization can be auditory or visual. Disruptions steal energy from getting the job done. Stopping to sort out stimulus from unexpected places reduces the Dark Energy we have available to attain our most precious goals.

Clutter is not just a physical thing. Our minds and spirits can also be cluttered. Think again about the filters mentioned under the "hearing" sensory indicator. What distractions are you carrying around that keep you from seeing clearly? What can you sort out and discard from your physical surroundings? From your emotional and mental surroundings? What habits of those in your inner circle cause you to use extra energy just to get around when working together?

If you can sense the clutter, so can others. Establish a culture of orderliness. This need not be a culture of Spartan or monastic simplicity. Surround yourself with objects and thoughts that positively impact your journey. Encourage others in your workplace to tidy up their offices, their thoughts, and their vision of the organization and of themselves.

- *What Am I Hearing?* As you walk through any organization you will hear how employees talk to each other and to customers. It is easy to pick up on the difference based on the tone of voice they use. You will also overhear how things are going in each part of the organization. When employees are content and things are going well, they are more engaged in their conversations and they sound happy.

  When things are not going well in an organization you will hear a change in the tone an employee uses when communicating. Their conversations are terse and short, almost daring the person they are communicating with "to start something." These employees need to blow off steam and just want an excuse to do it.

  While using your hearing sensory indicator, try to engage employees in conversations that focus on what is bothering them at that point in time. Keep the focus on current problems and avoid digging up past grudges. A small issue that could have been easily resolved will grow into a major dissatisfier if it is not addressed. Set yourself up with a regularly scheduled "listening tour." You will be surprised what you can hear about your organization's health. Hospitals do regular rounds to check on patients' progress and assure that good practices are being followed; you should do the same in your organization.

Reaching out as the executive gives you the ability to build relationships with others through empathy, listening, and authentic connection. Few things motivate employees more than knowing that the senior executive really listens to their needs, ideas, dreams, and complaints. Great leaders also know that the biggest payoff for improved listening may not be at work. It may be at home in the form of stronger relationships with their spouse, children, and friends.

Many leaders struggle with making time to listen because they believe the great myth: "I do not have time." However, effective leaders know that often "slower is faster." If you really want to resolve problems, taking ten minutes now to listen to the issue will save you hours in the long run. Why? Because you will get the full story and uncover the true dilemma. Ask your people: "Tell me more." When you hear what is going on, you'll make better decisions and achieve greater results.

The effective executive asks, "What do you need from me in order to feel comfortable speaking honestly?" The senior executive's listening and learning skills are emphasized. Any meeting in which the senior executive does lots of talking is followed by more meetings devoted to asking, "What did you hear and where did you come out?" The mode of operation is power-sharing, not power-taking or power-denying.

The sensory talent of "hearing" is a complex skill. We all listen through filters that have formed within us as we progress through life. These filters may be established through any number of experiences such as:

- Memories
- Expectations
- Physical environment
- Attitudes
- Beliefs
- Values
- Mores
- Prejudices

Executives in the public limelight must be cautious about how we filter what we hear from others. Filtering is a requirement of our position because of the immense amount of input we are subjected to on a daily basis. Knowing how to filter, analyze, and use the incoming information to make effective decisions is what keeps us in the top slot.

- *What Am I Feeling?* We all have had acid indigestion at some point in life and occasionally we get a sickening feeling about something in the organization that we know needs attention. It is hard to describe. We may be at a management meeting or retreat when we begin to experience that sinking feeling inside that things are not right. Feeling is one of our key management sensory indicators that must be monitored on a regular basis. If not, it can increase stress levels and affect health. Increased stress levels can make you appear flustered at meetings with employees, causing you to react quickly or abruptly to comments made by employees. If the stress levels increase enough it may impact your work in a negative way and make you look inefficient or even incompetent. If you let increased stress impact your work for long periods of time, you begin to become less productive; that is soon noticed by your superiors.

Sometimes we feel negative pressure building up in the organization, especially if there have been cutbacks and the remaining employees have been asked to pick up extra duties. Perhaps the company is doing poorly compared to its competitors and the pressure to improve immediately is intense. Or, there may be a general feeling of anxiety throughout the organization because of some top-management shakeups. Whatever is causing the negative pressure to build in the organization forces you and other employees onto a career rollercoaster. Everyone is thinking the same thing: "Should I stay and ride it out, or try to go to some place new and start over again?"

Malcolm Gladwell addresses the sensory indicator of feeling in his book *Blink*. It is about rapid cognition—the kind of thinking that happens in a blink of an eye. When you meet someone for the first time, or walk into a room for a meeting you are scheduled to lead, or read the first few sentences of a book, your mind takes about two seconds to jump to a conclusion about the situation around you. These instant conclusions are powerful and, occasionally, valuable. Another term for these conclusions is intuition. We use intuition to describe emotional reactions or gut feelings—thoughts and impressions that are generally not based on quantitative fact. Your intuition moves faster and operates more mysteriously than deliberate decision making.

No doubt you have become aware during your rise to executive leadership that your intuition is pretty good. You have come to believe that small voice inside you that tells you something beyond what the observable facts of a situation provide. This internal sensory scorecard is an important part of your executive tool kit. Learn to take advantage of that small voice. You may not always know where the conclusions come from that intuition hands you. If you think about it, you will realize that you have been counting on its presence for quite a while.

There is a subtle difference between the "feeling" sensory indicator described here and "sensing," the sensory indicator described next. Feeling is your personal emotional barometer working from within, reaching to the outside world to learn what is going on. Sensing is your personal external barometer, working from the outside world in to gauge the level of your internal awareness, the extent to which you are in tune with the outside world.

- *What Am I Sensing?* Many times you will not hear the problem but you will sense tenseness in the organization by observing the way people interact with one another. We have all been in the uncomfortable meeting where you could "cut the tenseness with a knife," but no one acknowledges the problem and the meeting ends with no resolution.

  Think about a time when you walked into a crowded room. You could not hear specific conversations coming from those already present, but the undercurrent in the room caused the hair on the back of your neck to rise. In another case, you instantly relaxed because you knew the event was a happy one. This sensing talent comes from the outside; it instantly connects with your internal antenna to help you assess the current situation.

  When you sense a difficult situation within your own organization, you must quickly scope out the relevant factors causing the discordance. Ask yourself what has happened recently within the organization that might be affecting the climate of the group with which you are interfacing. Have you just released a poor quarterly report? Has the national news broken the story of layoffs in one of your plants before you had the opportunity to make the announcement to the employees yourself?

Sometimes the tenseness is confined to a few individuals. You should address it with them in private to see whether you can resolve the issue before it spills over into other parts of the organization. Use your senior leadership team to help ferret out the details of your uncomfortable sensing experience. Be sure you develop a trusting relationship with at least two or three of your closest direct reports. When these situations arise, you can quietly discuss possible factors confident that the conversation won't spread beyond the corner office suite. If the situation involves someone from your inner circle, be extra careful about who you bring into your confidence. Remember, it is lonely at the top for a reason.

When you begin to sense a problem, confirm it by using your other senses to see whether it is a false alarm or just the beginning of something. Then use your ongoing quantitative measurement system to see whether what you are uncovering with your senses can be confirmed. You may uncover the need for different quantitative measurements if the current ones are not accurately depicting what you are uncovering with your sensory indicators.

- *What Does It Mean?* After you have done a regularly scheduled sensory tour of your organization, go back to your office and try to decide whether what you have heard, seen, felt, or sensed means something to yourself and your organization. Many times your sensory tour will be a positive experience; it will put you at ease that the organization is healthy and the employees engaged productively. Other times during these sensory tours something will attract your attention that can be implemented in other parts of the organization. It is always good to transfer internal best practices to help cross-fertilize the organization.

If you have responsibility for multiple facilities in different geographic locations, you must schedule sensory tours at all the locations. Then sort the information you collected by facility to see whether similarities or differences among the facilities can be identified.

These sensory tours need not be limited to your own organization. Take the time to visit suppliers, customers, competitors, and community partners. Get a solid feeling of how the different parts of your world work together. Make time to visit yourself. Relax and get to know your inner self. The time you take to become familiar with who you are is well worth it. The more surprises you spare yourself, the more time you can spend using your sensory indicators to move toward personal and organizational goals.

- *What Action Should I Take?* Most of the time, it won't be necessary to take any action. Just stay in monitoring mode. When you do uncover a problem or an issue that needs attention, you will have enough information from your sensory tours to guide you on the right course of action. By doing these tours you uncover problems that are simmering just under the surface. You won't be caught off guard by something that erupts with major consequences for the organization and the employees. It is better to know in advance what is happening, rather than wonder what happened after trouble starts. In essence, you should use these sensory tours as a guidepost to identify best practices. Something that works in one sector of the organization can be transferred to other sectors. Use the sensory tours to detect alarm signals that identify areas in need of attention; focus on those areas before they become wildfires that are difficult to control.

These sensory tours gather information for your internal scorecard; this will guide you when you begin to take action concerning your Executive Focus or to initiate a change in your organization. These measures will alert you that a transition zone is starting to appear on the horizon—for yourself or for your organization.

One thing we must all guard against is too much information from the same old sources. You know who they are: the ones who always complain, who are against anything new, and who are always in a negative mood. You must reach out broadly to get a reading on the pulse of the entire organization. Try to develop new sources for your sensory indicators that will give you information from a good cross-section of the organization. After a while you will tend to zero-in on a few reliable advisors.

10
Managing Workforce Talent

> - Are your human resources exiting at a rate faster than you can recruit new talent?
> - Do you lack a system to capture the knowledge of departing or retiring employees?
> - Are you unaware of what the strategic plan of the organization requires for talent over the next three to five years?
> - Do you lack a performance management system capable of capturing the data that would allow you to predict the talent development and training that you will need in the future?

If you answered "yes" to these questions, then you are not managing your human talent resources effectively to compete successfully in the future marketplace. In this chapter we discuss why the Human Resource department must focus on more than simply recruiting new employees to fill the void created by departing or retiring employees. Human Resources must begin to manage current human assets in order to increase retention and capture the knowledge that leaves with each departing employee.

The Human Resource department is charged with the task of managing the human talent assets of an organization. This encompasses the recruitment, retention, and development of people who embody the talent of the organization. If this management of talent assets is done correctly, it will give your organization an edge over your competition who are trying to hire fully trained, skilled, and talented professionals to fill their needs to compete successfully in the marketplace.

The baby boom workforce population is beginning a massive retirement process that will drain many thousands of workers from organizations. Those organizations will then have a difficult time finding adequate replacements. How large a drain does this represent in your organization? In your organization, the drain may be more pronounced in the executive and managerial ranks than in the general labor pool because the older workers have probably worked their way up the corporate ladder. When these older workers retire, they will take with them not only knowledge but also experience that is difficult to replace.

Consider an organization that manufactures a consumer product that has been a staple for many years. What happens when a key machinist retires? After 35 years, this machinist has seen numerous upgrades made to the equipment he operated. Because the organization has always been cost conscious, a lean engineering department made many revisions to the equipment that were not well documented. Because of this lean attitude, there was a fair amount of turnover in the engineering department. Over the years, this machinist ordered replacement parts from a metal fabricator that happened to be just a few miles from the plant. The same day the machinist retired, his contact at the metal fabricator also retired. Three weeks later the machine stopped working and the company ordered a replacement part. When the part was delivered it was found to be not even close to what was needed, but it was exactly what the blueprint for the machine indicated was correct. Both companies were forced to recall their retirees in order to get the right part made. Both companies incurred significant costs because of this situation. Both companies had lost knowledge and experience that they could not easily replace.

Successfully managing the exit of those retiring or leaving the organization for another job will be a key differentiator between success and failure in the future. Organizations must not let essential knowledge simply walk out the door. It is a waste of an asset and there is tremendous cost to replacing the talent that exits. Human Resources must ensure that there are systems in place that allow managers to capture the critical organizational knowledge of retiring or departing employees.

The Human Resource department must position itself in such a way that it is able to manage the human capital entrusted to it for the current and future benefit of the organization. It will not be sufficient to scour the marketplace for new talent to replace the talent that has left or is about to leave the organization. The Human Resource department must have its hand on the pulse of the organization's DNA. This DNA comprises the experience, education, knowledge, skills, creativity, and imagination of its employees. The Human Resource department must devise a strategy and plan to capture this DNA in a knowledge base that can be drawn upon by current and future workers.

Business writers are beginning to understand the negative consequences of not including the Human Resource function as an essential member of the executive team. Historically, the Human Resources Vice President has been a lower level member of the executive office. Rarely is Human Resources viewed as a core competitive component of the organization. The current talent management crisis is redefining the need for systematic integration of the planning function to permit the long-term development of skills, knowledge, and ability among employees.

Human Resources senior leadership has an expanded responsibility in strategic planning, organizational analysis, and system-level leadership. Unless the Human Resources senior leaders are accepted as equal to line senior management, their advice on talent management, recruitment, and hiring will not be valued and will not be implemented. This has serious long-term negative consequences for the organization. This expanded responsibility means that those climbing the Human Resources ladder will meet the same promotion and recognition challenges faced by other functional managers in the areas of Finance, Marketing, Engineering, Research and Development, or Operations.

The exodus of baby boomer employees highlights the cost of new employee recruitment, orientation, and training. Newer generations of workers are no longer loyal to a single employer for an entire career. Transportable benefit and retirement programs make it easy for an employee to move from job to job for career growth, rather than wait in line for promotion within a single company.

This increased turnover among higher-performing employees greatly raises recruitment and training expenses for the organization. Where once the challenge was to replace a poorly performing employee, the challenge now is to replace an excellent employee who leaves for a new position, taking along a plethora of skills and company knowledge.

The challenge for the Human Resource department is to answer the following questions:

1. *Future-State Talent Requirements:* What does the strategic plan indicate the talent need will be over the next three to five years in order to position the organization competitively?

2. *Current-State Talent Assessment:* What is the composition of our current workforce talent inventory? How does the current workforce talent inventory match up to the projected needs as outlined in the strategic plan?

3. *Gap Analysis:* What are the gaps between the current talent inventory and future talent requirements? What must we recruit and where should we focus our efforts?

4. *Talent Retention System:* Do we have a talent retention system that captures the operational and technical talent of our organization on an ongoing basis? If we do not already have such a system, can we develop one?

5. *Performance Management System:* Is our current performance management system capable of capturing the data on talent development we will need in the

future? Will our current performance management system provide the organization's senior management with the ability to understand current staffing resource levels and make projections for future needs?

6. *Risk Analysis:* Does the organization as a whole understand the risk of not investing in the management and retention of our workforce talent?

Once these questions have been answered, then the Human Resource department must focus on how to ensure that the organization is positioned for the future in order to actively manage its workforce talent. The three areas to focus on are current, retiring, and departing workers.

CURRENT WORKERS

The focus must be to organize the current-worker pool into knowledge areas. The first priorities are those critical managerial and technical skills that directly relate to the strategic direction of the organization. These are the most difficult to develop and replace. The Human Resource department must develop a system to help managers retain these critical employees and the organizational knowledge they possess.

Retaining these critical employees can be done by assuring that they are engaged in their work, that they receive the development and training they desire, and that the organization assists them with life and career planning.

Keeping employees fully engaged in their work does not seem to be working very well in the worldwide workforce today. According to a recent survey,[1] just one worker in five is engaged and ready to expend extra effort at work while thirty-eight percent are disenchanted. In Figure 10.1 we are able to view the various states of worker involvement in their current jobs. The degree of involvement with the work they are assigned is dependent upon the achievement of life and career goals that are important to each worker. It is obvious that everyone wants interesting work that is related to their life and career plans. When this is true, workers have high feelings of self-worth and this contributes to their life and work balance.

106 *Chapter Ten*

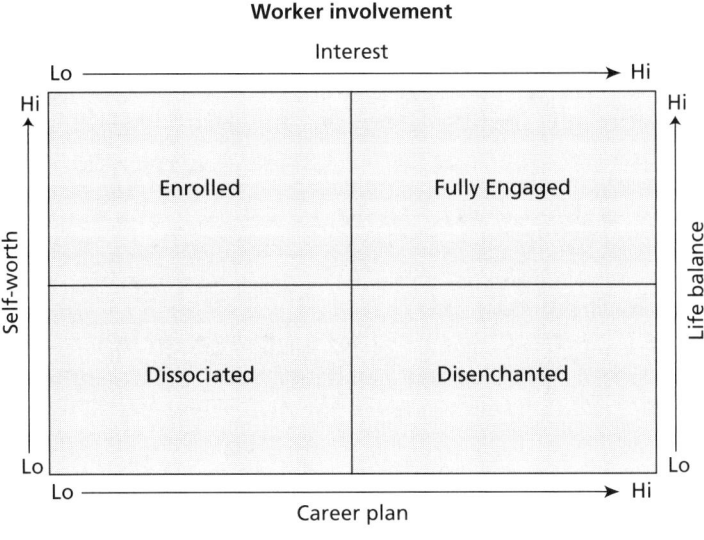

Figure 10.1 Engaged worker.

Human Resource departments must be aware of how employees are feeling about their work, and how that work contributes to life and career plans. Performance reviews must focus on the issues that are important to individual workers. Reviews must not simply document the happenings of the past twelve months. Workers are interested in what the future holds for them, not what happened in the past. Human Resource departments must provide managers with tools that will help them identify the level of worker involvement in their departments. Figure 10.1 illustrates four types of worker involvement:

- *Fully Engaged.* Happy in their environments, these workers feel that work is contributing to what they want in life and career. These employees are highly motivated; they feel connected to the organization. Even fully engaged employees will not operate in this category at all times. Everyone has routine work that must be done. This may drop them back to the *enrolled* category from time to time. Managers and employees must be aware of this movement between fully engaged and enrolled and address it only when the balance tips toward the enrolled mode more often than toward the engaged mode.

- *Enrolled.* The workers show up motivated every day but feel the work they are assigned is routine and uninteresting. They feel disconnected with their current work assignments and with their life and career plans. They probably are looking outside the organization for work that will make a connection with their life and career plans. It may take only some interesting and challenging team assignments or training to move these employees toward the fully engaged worker category. In order for this to happen, someone must monitor the workplace environment to identify those enrolled workers and then assist managers to re-engage them.

- *Disenchanted.* These workers are fed up with the organization and feel that what they do is not appreciated. They feel low self-worth and may not have a good balance between work and life. They frequently complain, but they are not heard. They possess skills and knowledge that are not being utilized. Sometimes people who are close to retirement and who have achieved their life and career plans wind up in this category. Workers in this category are being wasted in spite of the knowledge and experience they have that can benefit the organization. When people in this category leave the organization, replacing them comes at a significant recruitment cost. Rather than spending recruitment dollars, it would be wiser to identify disenchanted employees and help them improve their work conditions and become enrolled and engaged once again. If work conditions are a factor, recruitment dollars are wasted to find someone new who will leave for the same reasons.

- *Dissociated.* This worker is totally unattached from the organization. Dissociated employees feel no need to expend effort. They may have frequent absences and work short days. Often senior employees in this category feel untouchable. If they have a history of making trouble for past managers, current managers may not challenge them to perform. If no one expects anything from them, dissociated workers become a drag on the organization. They must be dealt with or they will begin to infect others with their negative attitudes.

DEPARTING WORKERS

Departing workers should be interviewed in order to learn what motivated them to leave. Was it the work? Was it conflict with management? Pay and benefits? Perhaps it was lack of advancement opportunity or lack of training and development? Or it may have been something else entirely. It is important to understand why a departing worker is leaving. Systems must be put in place to correct what is causing departures and retain those who are still employed. Efforts should be made to assess what knowledge and skills are leaving with them. Has this knowledge been captured so that others will be able to step up and do the job? If not, how will that work be accomplished? Many of today's jobs are technology-based; when workers depart, they take with them technology "secrets." This secret system knowledge may include shortcuts they developed, quick fixes for hardware that goes down frequently, network configurations that are not written down anywhere, critical data analysis spreadsheets they developed, and so on. If this knowledge is not captured and retained, the organization will have to recreate it, and that can be costly.

RETIRING WORKERS

Retiring workers have a tremendous amount of historic organizational knowledge, the base upon which the organization was built. The Human Resource department must identify those nearing retirement age and work with managers to capture their knowledge before it's too late. Employees retiring from critical knowledge areas could be offered staff or mentoring assignments that would help the organization position itself for the future. Sometimes using retiring employees as mentors for those who replace them can help both parties achieve life and career goals.

The Human Resource department should be developing an end-of-career system to make the transition of knowledge, responsibility, and skills a seamless and rewarding process for the retiring employee. This system should be a value-recognition event that will increase retiring employees' feelings of self-worth and keep them motivated until retirement.

Because expertise may be difficult and costly to replace in the labor market, organizations must learn to be creative with retiring critical-skill employees. In the near future, organizations will need to experiment with different work structures in order to retain these critical skills and to effectively compete for scarce labor talent. Organizations may offer retiring employees guaranteed consulting contracts for one to two years to keep them on call in case they are needed. The consulting work could include mentoring younger managers, working on short-term projects, documenting knowledge application areas, heading up interim assignments, evaluating future markets, and so on. However these future work structures develop, they must be actively managed by Human Resources so that available skills are matched to organizational needs. Just setting the system up and letting it run itself will result in disaster and unexpected costs. This new work structure will have a labor pool that must be included in strategic planning for future human resource needs. Some creative organizations that develop a critical talent pool of retired labor may outsource them to other organizations and enjoy a return on the financial investment.

The focus of this chapter has been on new ways of managing human talent resources effectively in order to compete successfully in the marketplace of the future. In this chapter we discussed the need for the Human Resource department to focus away from simply recruiting new talent to fill the void created by departing or retiring employees. Instead, it must begin to manage current human assets of the organization in order to increase retention and capture the knowledge that leaves with each departing employee. This expanded Human Resources responsibility will require its senior managers take a more integrated role within the organization. They must prove their value as peers of senior line managers, as critical strategic thinkers and leaders.

It is time to get away from year-end performance reviews that look at only what happened in the past. We must move to regular reviews that focus on whether employees are achieving their life and career plans. Organizations that help their employees achieve life and career goals will have better retention rates and more satisfied employees. Satisfied and productive workers are the best recruitment force you can have to attract the critical human talent an organization needs to compete in the future. It will always be less costly to an organization to retain rather than recruit.

Note

1. Just 1 in 5 workers are engaged and most want more from executives, Andrea Coombes, *Market Watch*, October 21, 2007

11
Multi-Generational Teams Need Focus, Too

- Do your employees look out for themselves first, before they look out for their teammates and the company?
- Do your teams have problems with conflicting cultures, hot buttons, and preferred ways of doing things?
- Do teams begin projects and then fade away into other activities without providing results?
- Do you have real teams, or are they just groups of individuals looking busy?
- Do supervisors pull rank by removing employees from team assignments for "more important short-term activities"?
- Is finger pointing more prevalent in your teams than hand raising?

If you answered "yes" to these questions, then you are not using teams effectively to meet the competitive needs of your business or your customers. Successful teams act like successful families, with a relationship based on interdependence and mutual trust and support. Teams are most successful meeting company goals when they are clearly focused on key drivers and outcomes required by your major customers.

Teams can help with your Executive Focus by giving you a means with which to pull together diverse parts of the organization. Teams can work on priorities that are important to you and your organization. Teams can help reduce stress by cutting across organizational boundaries, and by improving communications and work processes that are not meeting customer needs and expectations.

An executive who becomes skilled at using teams to accomplish organizational goals and objectives understands the benefits of employee involvement. Having an active teaming process allows executives to broaden the scope of their sensory skills. Cross-functional teams cut through divisional and functional silos to shorten communication and feedback channels.

Teams become a microcosm of the organization and present a blended indicator of its health. A solid team culture provides a sounding board for the executive to use in assessing the results of ongoing initiatives. This sounding board can also be used to articulate doubt and explore objective ways to overcome it. Having this sounding board helps the executive feel less isolated and stressed.

The attitudes of team members reflect the overall feeling within the organization, especially during times of rapid change and stress. Team members are generally more willing to speak their minds and they hold a higher opinion of themselves and the organization. Team members are usually chosen because of their skills and abilities. They are recognized as strong contributors who will honestly assess the situation. They are usually willing to acknowledge doubt and to identify solutions in a positive manner.

THE NEW TEAM MAKEUP

Executives must realize that teams today are different than they were in the past. Teams today are more diverse and may include members from various countries, cultures, and generations. Today we have multi-generational teams composed of baby boomers, Generation Xers, and Millenials. Each of these generations brings to the team unique experiences, expectations, educations, and technical abilities. The younger workers may be experienced at multi-tasking, a skill acquired during their college years. They may attend a meeting and be text messaging on an unrelated topic at the same time. This can appear rude to other generations but it is acceptable to theirs. Baby boomers finally got comfortable with e-mail, and now must learn text messaging and the abbreviated language used within it. Baby boomers become upset when Millenial workers ignore e-mail, preferring to use text messaging only. Remember when people would not return your voicemail messages because they only used e-mail and you were confused by that?

These multi-generational teams are a new hurdle that team leaders must now contend with, along with the common problems and difficulties always present when teams are formed by senior management and chartered to accomplish a task. This chapter will focus on techniques to deal with both new and common challenges leaders face when guiding a team to a successful project conclusion.

HOW TO BUILD EFFECTIVE TEAMS

Building and maintaining effective teams is not easy. Individuals have brains, ideas, and energy. Orchestrating these individual characteristics into a common focus is often more difficult than herding cats.

Chapter 10 discussed the major issues of retention and engagement of skilled employees. This chapter explores the challenge of engaging employees not only in the goals of the organization, but in those goals as a community of interrelated skills, talents, and results.

Individuals leverage their personal skills by sharing them with others. Ideas are like love: the more you give away, the more you get. An idea that sits in one person's mind may be simply a good one. But shared and evolved through dynamic discussion, that idea expands exponentially into a successful competitive edge for your company. These ideas find fertile ground with teams, where they are cultivated and harvested as marketable outcomes for the business.

For teams to be successful, the individuals making up the team must see that more value will accrue to them as a result of working with others than would accrue to them working alone. Those who are secure in their own worth are more likely to look outward for additional accomplishment. Abraham Maslow (1943) identified a needs hierarchy in which humans have a variety of different needs. These can be classified into five specific groups and then arranged in a hierarchy of importance.

Figure 11.1 recreates Maslow's Needs Hierarchy. At the bottom are the *physiological needs*—the things we need to survive. In the workspace, adequate wages for food and clothing, reasonable working conditions, and so forth are generally thought to satisfy these needs. Next are *security needs,* which reflect the desire to have a safe physical and emotional environment. Third in the hierarchy are the needs for *belongingness*. These include the desire for love and affection and the need to be accepted by our peers. *Esteem needs* come next. These comprise two different sets: the need for recognition and

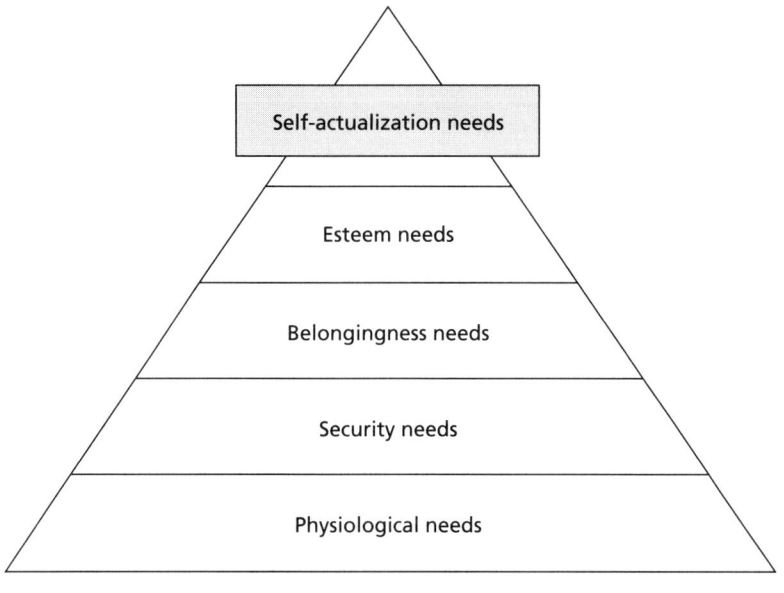

Figure 11.1 Maslow's needs hierarchy.

respect from others, and the need for self-respect and a positive self-image. Finally, at the top of the hierarchy are the *self-actualization needs*—the need to continue to grow, develop, and expand our capabilities. Opportunities to participate, take on increasingly important tasks, and learn new skills may all lead to satisfaction of these needs.

Organizations wishing to get the most out of high-performing teams must provide for the basic physiological and security needs before individuals can focus on the higher level behaviors associated with belongingness, self-esteem, and growth. Human perception is critical in the leadership of teams. Although the workplace may be physically safe, if the individual does not feel safe from reprisal, unwarranted termination, or other capricious actions on the part of management, they will not be effective in teams. They will be constantly looking over their shoulders for the unexpected. There will be little trust or commitment to the organization.

The physiological and security needs discussed above are the underpinnings of most life and career plans that individuals on the team have developed and are pursuing. If they find that the teamwork they are undertaking supports their lives and career achievement/avoidance goals, they will be productive and committed team members.

ELEMENTS OF EFFECTIVE TEAMS

Chapter 10 introduced a 2 x 2 matrix to illustrate worker involvement and engagement. Figure 10.1 combined continuums of interest, self-worth, life-balance, and career plan to illustrate levels of employee enrollment, engagement, disenchantment, and dissociation. This same concept works well for effective teams.

A major tactic for engaging individuals into teams is to gain commitment to a common purpose. Military texts and business books point to the need for clear goals, direct feedback on results, and immediate reinforcement of gains as solidifying factors in teams. Table 11.1 offers a list of elements that are proven techniques to focus teams on the long-term success of your organization and your customer's needs.

Table 11.1 Elements of an effective team.

Element	Supporting activity
Identify an overarching common purpose.	Make sure organizational goals are clearly understood by the team.
	Involve team members in identifying the highest priorities for team outcomes.
	Establish clear team goals based on those priorities and tie them directly to the major goals of the organization.
Clearly identify roles and responsibilities of each team member.	Engage the team members in defining their roles within the first two team meetings.
	Keep in touch with team members to be sure their individual roles are understood, especially if those roles change as the team progresses.
	Use the technique of shared leadership to instill true accountability and empowerment among team members.
	Exhibit strong leadership by encouraging informed risk and innovation within the team.
Encourage trust within the team by trusting the team.	Instill an environment of mutual respect.
	Share information at all costs. If something is truly confidential, be clear about why.
	Create a climate of interdependency among team members.
	Show that you trust the team members.
	Support the team when they question or disagree with an idea; listen carefully to new ideas.
Define and respect consistent processes and procedures.	Establish well-defined team methods of operation in early team meetings.
	Cultivate outstanding team problem-solving techniques.
	Develop clear measures of team success.
Get results.	Drive for outstanding team results.
	Celebrate team synergy when it happens.
	Leverage optimized skills, talents, and resources.
	Learn what gives the team satisfaction and produces commitment.
	Create a team culture of inclusion, passion, and customer focus.

Continued

Table 11.1 Elements of an effective team. *Continued*

Element	Supporting activity
Provide growth opportunities for all team members.	Exhibit a commitment to continuous learning.
	Be flexible and adaptive in rewarding team members as they expand their contributions to the team and the organization.
	Provide ongoing objective assessments of team members and the team as a whole.
Define technology the team will utilize.	At the first meeting, decide which technology platform the team will use.
	Ensure all team members know how to use it.
	Provide training for those not proficient in the technology.
	Utilize only the technology chosen by the team and insist all use it for team communications.
	Give all other electronics a rest during the team meeting.

The elements in Table 11.1 focus on a combination of process and human factors involved in effective team engagement. Common purpose, defined roles and responsibilities, processes, and procedures are part of an operational framework that empowers individuals and holds them accountable for the results of the project. Trust and growth are behavioral characteristics that solidify the motivational environment in which teams thrive and succeed.

Other valuable characteristics of effectively focused teams are:

- Attention to detailed elements of work
- Teamwork that is integrated into the daily routine
- Members who work together toward common goals
- A team that remains intact project after project
- A focus on incremental improvement
- A commitment to measured financial and operational results

Focus teams on important goals by providing a "direct line of sight" from the strategic business plan to the front-line working level of the organization. Alignment of team activity to the key drivers of the organization is an effective way to maintain focus on what is important to both customer and executive leadership. Humans are generally goal driven. Clearly identify what is most important within the workplace. Publish the goals and objectives of the organization, and share the key measurements that management is accountable for. Reward the attainment of those goals across all levels of the workforce.

Cross-functional project teams are a challenge to maintain because individuals within the team report to different first-line managers. As job requirements change and operational crises arise, a manager may be tempted to "borrow" an employee back from responsibility to a team. Team members who are committed to the results of the team and who have a clear understanding of the value of team outcomes can reinforce the need for their continued involvement in the cross-functional team. Senior management must support the inclusion of individuals on teams outside of their departments and stand up to line managers who succumb to the temptation to pull individuals back for short-term department activities.

TECHNOLOGY AND TEAMS

To make these new multi-generational teams work effectively, the team leader must establish rules for the technical culture in which teams now operate. The diversity of technology available to teams is enormous and some team members will be more fluent in the use of advanced technology than others. This can be a cause of conflict within a team.

It is important that the team develop and agree to policies regarding a common use of technology. Some simple technology rules will help reduce conflicts within the team:

- Cell phones to be off at team meetings; no text messaging.
- No game playing while we are meeting as a team.
- Turn off iPods during team meetings.

- Members will abide by a team decision regarding which electronic medium will be used to send meeting minutes and other relevant documents—text or e-mail.
- All members will use the pre-determined medium for communication between meetings.
- All team members are to be proficient and comfortable with the technology the team will be utilizing.
- Team members who need training will get it. Inability to use the team's chosen technology will be a source of conflict down the road.

BEHAVIOR AND TEAMS

The multigenerational team can be a powerful one within an organization, but managing such a team is more difficult because there is such a wide range of knowledge, skills, experience, culture, and technology utilization. There is also a wide range of behavior, ranging from the more conservative to the apparently rude. This can be a source of conflict unless it is addressed and harnessed at the beginning of the team's existence. Each generation on the team has its own priorities, hot buttons, preferred ways of doing things, and ethics. The process of blending this wide range of preferences begins at the first team meeting. Many of the members may find difficulty working effectively with others because of the possibility for generational clashes of ideals and culture. One way to handle this is to think of how you keep peace at a Thanksgiving dinner table that may include up to four generations. Rather than letting individuals sit in like groups, assign seating so that everyone has a chance to meet the others and talk. Don't let the meeting room break up into generational pockets. Keep the smaller groups mixed and productive. Broach the topic of multi-generational teams at the start of the first meeting. Let everyone know that the team has a major problem to solve, and that the solution will be delayed by behavioral problems that might result if generational or cultural differences interfere with the group's ability to work together effectively and efficiently.

TEAMS AND INNOVATION

Teams become a hotbed for innovation: "Necessity is the mother of invention." Teams who are clear on project goals, who understand their roles and responsibilities, and who command the skills necessary to deliver the required outcomes are a major creative force within the organization. Individuals are stronger when we leverage ideas with the ideas and opinions of others. Research institutions, conferences, and symposia are all based on healthy debate surrounding the generation of new ideas, the questioning of those ideas by others, and the synthesis of new ideas as a result of open dialog.

Encourage creative conflict as a vehicle for teasing out unspoken ideas from your workforce. Team members may be reluctant to share ideas in which they are highly invested for fear of ridicule and judgment. An open environment of celebrating differences makes it appropriate to offer disparate thoughts. It is better to deal with the occasional personality dispute that occurs during open disagreement than to miss the opportunity of hearing ideas that surface along with the emotional exchange.

What transforms a group of employees into an effective team? When a group creates its own sense of community, it becomes more than a congregation of individuals. It becomes an interconnected team working toward common goals. Compare the following characteristics of effective groups with the list of team elements in Table 11.1:

- Group goals must be clearly understood and relevant.
- Members must be committed to the group goals.
- Group members must communicate their ideas and feelings.
- Participation and leadership must be distributed among members.
- Appropriate decision-making procedures must be used flexibly.
- Power and influence must be approximately equal throughout the group.

- Conflicts arising from opposing ideas and opinions are encouraged.
- Group cohesion must be high.
- Problem-solving adequacy must be high.
- The interpersonal effectiveness of members must be high.

There is a close match between the elements of an effective team and the characteristics of groups that work well together. Groups may work together in ongoing situations without first having been organized into formal teams. Departments become high-performing teams by using the elements of good teamwork even in the absence of formal team orientation.

Building and maintaining teams is a multi-faceted activity. It is a combination of process and behavior. Goals, charters, ground rules, and effective meetings are only part of what makes a team effective. Emphasis on charters, empowerment, self-direction, or coaching can't fix broken relationships. At the most basic level, team success depends on the best of human nature, not merely on shared business goals. If we appeal to and reinforce rewarding human relationships, our objectives will be accomplished.

The concept of effective teams is much like the concept of an effective family. Families are interdependent. Families share more than the roof over their heads. Families don't just work together; they care about each other. Teams, like families, are engaged in valuable, common goals. Individuals are secure in their self-worth and maintain a life-balance beyond their identities within the team. Some of the most human supports for a team are closely related to the concept of family:

- *Nobody is perfect.* Everyone has skills and shortcomings. Play to the positive and redirect the negative. Find out what team members do best and help them succeed in that role.
- *If you have special knowledge that someone else can use, share it.* There is no place on a business team for showoffs. If you can help someone else, do it without expecting special recognition.

- *Family comes first.* When a family member is ill or a child needs a parent at school, team members should be free to leave work immediately. Team members should not work if they are themselves ill. A successful team meets individual physiological and security needs. Conversely, individuals must be there when the team needs them.

- *Cover for each other.* If a team member is unable to complete a task, the team will close ranks and pick up the slack. The team must be judged as a group, not as individuals.

Another perspective that is useful for leading teams is to understand why some teams don't work. Teams are like individuals; we are social creatures. We don't work well when we are isolated. Teams are more effective when they are closely connected to a company-wide effort or at least directly tied to major outcomes of the organization.

Teams need to know they can rely on champions and sponsors within the organization for resources and timely decision-making. When resources are redirected, when team members are pulled from the project for short-term activities, or when other support is redirected from critical activities, the team quickly realizes that it is not trusted or valued by the company. When key management personnel move about too frequently and workgroups are not provided with consistent leadership and management support, the teams lose the focus and energy necessary to achieve results.

Management can support effective teams in a number of ways:

- *Communicate and listen.* Encourage two-way, honest, open, frequent communication. Be available for new ideas, resolution of conflict, and recognition of significant milestones.

- *Train employees.* If employees don't know what to do, how to do it right, or, most important, why it is done a certain way and what difference it makes, you can't expect them to feel or act empowered. Work with the team leader to understand and support the growth requirements of team members.

- *Team employees.* No one has found a technological alternative to cooperation when it comes to building a positive work climate. Help the team identify outside subject matter experts for short-term support or special information requirements. Exhibit strong team behaviors among the executive ranks as a model for operational teams.

- *Trust employees.* Support team decisions even when they aren't the outcomes you had in mind. Trust teams with information and allow them to fail. As team champion or sponsor, your responsibility is to provide the "why" of the outcome. Allow the team to suggest the "how" that gets to the result.

- *Feedback.* Recognize efforts as well as results by finding frequent and creative ways to say thank you. Share the glory in every way possible. Give frequent, specific performance feedback that is both positive and constructive.

Identifying the type of team process or activity can be very useful. Too often, team sponsors or champions assume that a team is just a set of activities waiting to be automated. Team sponsors need a broad enough view of team activities that they can see some of the sub-processes going on within the team. Put a different way: all important teams include sub-team activities performed by people!

Teams work on processes that support the organization. These processes may be automated, repeatable, and even within some level of statistical control. One of the major activities within teams is mapping the processes under improvement or study. Any process diagram that shows only activities to be automated is probably so far from the concerns of managers or customers that it wouldn't be a view that managers or customers can relate to. Teams of individuals working together are what make processes function effectively. It is the human element of the team that draws the attention of managers and customers.

Recognize that the team itself is as important to the organization as the outcomes of team activity. Engagement of individuals into high-performing teams provides more value to the organization than the results of team activity. Managers and customers not only see the tangible results of team success, they also experience the behaviors and attitudes of team members. When individuals are excited about their involvement in company activities, it comes across in their interactions with others. This positive attitude is catching. Peers catch the excitement; customers see the energy.

This energy is created no matter what task the team is assigned. It is important, however, to appropriately match the needs of the individual with the focus of the team. Some individuals prefer a stable, organized workplace. There is great need in the organization for those who can maintain interest in routine activities that can be precisely defined in advance. Many tasks in the workplace are highly repetitive. Most operations in traditional corporations are prescribed and standardized. Asking teams to take the lead on providing consistently high outputs is an empowering opportunity for individual and team growth.

Collaborative activities that involve creating first an exact sub-process to be followed and then outputs that cannot be defined in advance offer more visibility. This type of activity requires a team of creative people to analyze a problem. It isn't an activity that is likely to be automated, highly repetitive, or standardized. When the essence of the activity is that people solve a problem that cannot be precisely defined in advance, creativity and innovation are critical characteristics of the team.

Getting the right individuals on the right team is important. Rapid change and the conflicts that ensue are exciting to some. To others, it is a stress generator. When the right people are included on a team, they willingly engage in activities focused on team goals. When individuals are mismatched, they are more easily distracted by uncomfortable changes. Their sense of belonging is threatened because they are not in consonance with the activities around them. Their self-esteem is challenged by the reality of their discomfort. Even one mismatched team member can create discordance strong enough to break apart a well-performing team.

Teams provide the energy for Executive Focus. Use the human aspect of teams to drive the company forward to higher levels of competitive achievement. Choose the right individuals to be on the team. Support them with skills, knowledge, and resources to get the job done. Recognize the team as a whole for results. Recognize individuals for their involvement and support to the team. Share the success of the organization with the teams who get you there. Success breeds success. Focus on what matters. Focus on your teams and the individuals who commit to making those teams a critical part of your organization.

Teams enhance Executive Focus by expanding an executive's ability to more comprehensively assess the health of the organization. Once we understand the health of our organization, we can better clarify our choices for the future.

12

Pause–Relax–Refresh

- Do you feel that you are always at work – never out of touch?
- Do you feel that you are falling behind the rest of your co-workers?
- Do your co-workers behave badly to each other?
- Do you feel so stressed that you might explode?

If you answered "yes" to these questions, then you are definitely in the new world of work. In this new world of work, speed is the most important commodity. We must go faster in order to make more time for the tasks we wish to accomplish. In this chapter we focus on techniques that will help you proportion your time and give you a balanced perspective on what shape your current life is in and what must be done to improve it.

FASTER AND FASTER

There seems to be a conspiracy in our culture to see how fast we can make people do things. We are never out of reach of subtle psychological signals, such as sounds or colors, that make us go faster and faster. When we get up in the morning we can watch "Know and Go" news. On the way to work we stop for gasoline and see the "Pump and Go" sign; wave your magic card and you get gas and a bill. If we stop for breakfast, it's at "On the Go." Lunch is at "Lunch on the Run"' pantry; at the bank we have express lines and drive-by ATMs; for dinner we can have "Express Meals;" and to finish off the day we can stop at "Rapid Refill" to pick up what we need for the evening. On the weekend we can get "Workaholic Batteries" for our garden tractor. Everywhere we turn we must move as fast as a speeding bullet or we are perceived to be falling behind the power curve. And we wonder why we are stressed!

We used to make fun of geeks with pocket protectors full of pens and pencils. How many of you today carry a cell phone, BlackBerry, pager, Nextel sky phone, iPod, and more? Recently one of the authors saw a man at an airport wearing all these things on his belt. In addition, he carried a heart monitor to record his stress levels. It doesn't take a doctor to see that the cure for his heart condition is simple: get rid of everything else on the belt! All of these technology gadgets are designed to keep us in touch with our workplace so we can always be available.

Because of all these technology marvels, it's possible to be "at work" 24/7. If we could find more hours in the day, we would probably fill them up with even more tasks. We are constantly in touch with our subordinates and our bosses, and we tend to be involved with every detail of every decision being made, no matter how minor. We have gone deep into an information age where every little detail is analyzed to death. Recently one of the national news stations showed a car chase in California for 6 hours until it came to a dramatic end. Throughout the chase the news station had guest commentators analyzing everything the police were doing—how they were pursuing the vehicle, how they might stop it, what they might do if they did stop it, and how they would handle the suspect when they caught him. A suspect with a television in his car would have had real-time consulting advice on to how escape. Do we really need this much information every day on every topic?

This constant on-the-go mentality is taking its toll on the workforce by adding more and more daily stress. Unfortunately, we do not digest this faster-and-faster psychology well. Instead, what we observe and experience is that we and our co-workers have increased stress at work. This increased stress manifests itself in a number of ways that are not productive to a successful working environment. We see many of the following on a regular basis:

- *Projectiles.* Things being thrown by frustrated workers at a wall or a person because some deadline was missed or because a project is being completed late.
- *Damage.* Equipment being damaged by rage, especially computer monitors, because items are deemed too slow or not instantly responsive.
- *Loud language.* People shouting at others or over others in meetings in order to get their points of view heard.
- *Rudeness.* Rude language or gestures displayed as part of a conversation about a work-related project in which some members of the team are not doing their fair share of the work involved.
- *Cubical confrontations.* People having complete meltdowns over the way others are behaving in their cubicles and how that behavior interferes with the ability to get work accomplished.
- *Aggression.* Someone gets pushed or hit during a dispute over who should be doing what.
- *Flame mail.* An e-mail attacking individuals for lack of cooperation or teamwork on a project is sent to everyone in the organization. This kind of behavior identifies a person who has been totally stressed-out and can take no more.

Because of all the information coming at us from outside and inside the workplace, we often feel paralyzed and stressed-out when making a decision. We are overloaded with mountains of data and opinions about what should be done or what future action should be taken. We know that new information will appear as soon as we make a decision that we may want to reconsider. Someone will second-guess us. We tend to be stressed-out by this barrage of information that is constantly coming at us, to the point that we avoid our incoming e-mail.

Because our subordinates are also influenced by this information overload, they forward everything to be sure we are on board and up to date. Like it or not, you are probably micromanaging your subordinates and your bosses are doing the same to you. It's no wonder that at the end of each day you feel as though nothing was accomplished—and there are still fifty unread e-mail messages in your in box. Many of us have come to feel that we only accomplish something when there is a crisis and that often the wrong things get done.

In order to keep our Executive Focus, each of us must begin a process of unraveling this information that is coming at us constantly. Several techniques can help reduce stress caused by this overload:

- *Eliminate "make work."* Always be on guard for the "make work" executive. This is the person we've seen running down the hall with tons of file folders, heading to every meeting in the building. He tells anyone who will listen that he is involved in some top-level project and that he needs data from you and others instantly and continuously. He will analyze and forward this data up the line so an important decision can be made. These "make work" executives involve themselves in everything they possibly can in an effort to make themselves invaluable to the organization.

  These people are constantly running spreadsheets to analyze data and they always need more data to populate the never-ending and expanding spreadsheets. They are in early and they leave late because there is so much to do. When they are terminated or they move on, all the "vital" work they were doing just stops and no one picks up any of it. You receive no more requests for the essential data you were sending for the big decision that was to be made with that input. What they were doing was "make work" to justify their existence. No one dared challenge them since they seemed to be empowered by some higher authority to get this done. These "make work" executives are clever at disguising that they have no real authority to make requests from others. They are clever at suggesting that they have been empowered to get this job done and at appearing reluctant to "be forced to tell anyone that you did not cooperate." They often are able to fool those above them into thinking they have this top-level empowerment. They will stop top-level executives in the hallways to discuss something just so others will see them, and will position themselves at meetings to always be near the power source. They will volunteer for any assignment just to get closer to the top. This is all in an effort to legitimize their "make work" position.

Be on guard for these "make work" executives; always question what they are asking from you to be sure it is legitimate. Ask where they are sending the data and what they are using it for. Tell them you will call whomever they say they are reporting to for this project, just to be sure this is what they really want and need. The more questions you ask, the less likely they will be to bother you because they do not want themselves exposed. The more questions you ask, the faster they will replace you with someone they can con into responding to their requests for "make work" information. Use this strategy to effectively manage your workload by eliminating the "make work" workload of another executive.

- *Exercise.* Give your mind a rest. Start doing some type of regular exercise that you enjoy. There are many types of exercise available, from yoga to sports to simply going for a walk at lunch. Exercise will reduce muscle tension, improve the blood flow to your brain, and release endorphins into your blood, giving you a feeling of euphoria or happiness. Anything that can relieve work stress will help overall productivity. Plan this into your daily schedule and adhere to it as carefully as you do your regularly scheduled meetings.

- *Sleep.* Some executives need more than five hours of sleep a night. Organize your leadership team and game plan so that you can leave the office, attend necessary evening functions, hang up the tux or high heels, and go to bed at a reasonable hour. By now you know how much sleep you need to function. Plan your schedule so you get it.

- *Take a deep breath.* Proper breathing is the basis of yoga and other Eastern meditation styles. A full-lung inhale and exhale is restoring to both the body and the mind. Breathe in and exhale slowly several times a day. Schedule it as a mid-morning and mid-afternoon habit.

- *Focus on accomplishments.* Take pride in what you have done and not what is left to do. During every workday make a list of what you accomplished – no matter how small. An accomplishment is an accomplishment. Praise yourself. Your psyche and your health will appreciate it.

- *Get out of e-mail management detail.* You don't need every detail. Tell subordinates to do their jobs and keep you informed on the big picture. Once you open the door to reading and responding to every e-mail from your subordinates, they just keep coming faster and faster. Control the flow.

- *Clean house.* Return to Chapter 5 and think again about organizational and personal clutter. What causes you unnecessary disruption? Throw it out, recycle it, re-mission it to a more productive place in the organization or in your life. Stop walking around with the "stuff" that drains away pieces of Dark Energy that you need elsewhere.

- *Laugh and have fun.* You are leading the organization because you enjoy it…or, at least, you used to. Pause, relax, and refresh. Circle the wagons again and take care of yourself. You are worth it.

- *Self inspection.* Regularly revisit your personal SWOT from Chapter 4. Where are your strengths? What can you do over the next three days to play on one of those strengths? What weaknesses did you identify? Are they still valid after some period of time? Congratulate yourself if you have stepped over a hurdle. Schedule action to resolve a weakness and get it out of the way for good.

Now that you have developed a routine to help you relax, it's time to decide how to best utilize your refreshed self. Focus on the four pillars of this book:

1. Your organization's needs
2. Your career needs
3. Your job needs
4. Your personal needs

Be sure you are proportioning your time appropriately over all four of the pillars to give yourself a balanced perspective on your current life and what must be done to get it in better shape.

13
Summary: Now What?

- Do you still have career goals to achieve?
- Do you still drag yourself to work each day?
- Do you still feel not engaged in your work?
- Do you still feel out of alignment with your organization?
- Do you still feel that something is missing in your life?

If you answered "yes" to these questions, then this chapter will help you regain your Executive Focus so work can once again become enjoyable and rewarding. You must develop strategies and begin the process of regaining balance between your life and career that you seek but haven't yet achieved. The new world of work is difficult to navigate without the appropriate focus and strategy to achieve the goals you desire.

NOW WHAT?

What will you do with the rest of your career? It's a major question and you owe yourself an answer. It's a question we should all be asking ourselves on a regular basis in order to keep what is important front-of-mind at all times.

In order to answer the big question, we must first answer these small questions:

- What is it I want out of my current career?
- What is it I am not getting out of my current career?
- Can I obtain what I want in my current position or organization?
- If I cannot obtain what I want, where should I go?
- What strategy should I use to obtain what I need and want?

These are the key questions we must ask ourselves. A gap analysis will allow us to look at what we want and what we have achieved. The larger the gap, the more intently we should be working to close it. A large gap is a major dissatisfier that can slowly build up stress and unhappiness within us if we do not reduce its impact. In order to regain our Executive Focus we must answer two sets of needs questions honestly. What is it we need and want, and to what degree are we determined to succeed?

There are *survival needs:*

- What are the financial resources I desire?
- What are the organizational positions I want?
- What kind of power do I want?
- What kind of visibility do I want?
- How much stress am I willing to handle?
- What type of work do I need to keep me engaged and motivated?
- Do my values match up with the organization's values?

There are *emotional needs:*

- What kind of trust do I want from my co-workers and bosses?

- What knowledge and proficiency must I achieve to remain current?
- What will improve my self-esteem and keep it high?
- What type of involvement do I need to keep me engaged and productive?
- What type of acknowledgement will make me feel fulfilled and from whom must it come?

In order to achieve our goals, we must look inside ourselves and understand whether we can remain adequately motivated, engaged, and pumped up to maintain the necessary drive. You present yourself to the world from the inside out. Remember the old saying "if you can fake sincerity, you can fool anyone" only works for so long. It takes more energy to fake it than it does to really do it on a regular basis. Fakers always get caught because they run out of energy.

Executive Focus on the right track is fueled by a Dark Energy that thrives on the right attitude of a highly motivated person. The right attitude runs on a platform focused by a value proposition that you have clearly defined for yourself. You have developed a value proposition that lets you balance your needs—what is in it for you—with the needs of the organization—what is in it for them.

KEEPING YOURSELF MOTIVATED AND ENGAGED

How do we keep ourselves motivated, engaged, and pumped up on a day-to-day basis so we can achieve personal Executive Focus goals while still executing our strategy? There are many ways to do this:

- *Go with the flow when trapped in a transition zone.*
  This is a simple strategy to follow when executing your Executive Focus plan. You know that important things cannot be achieved overnight; they take time. Be happy where you are by focusing on the positives of your current position, the things that are helping

you achieve some of the needs and wants you desire. Use the glass-is-half-full philosophy to stay motivated.

- *Keep pace with your competitors (peers) as you chase similar goals.* Watch what they do and imitate what works. Improve your knowledge level, get involved with major organizational initiatives, do some volunteer work, or volunteer to lead a project team that's forming around an organizational problem.

- *Analyze your current situation to try to understand the causes of your stress, not just the symptoms.* Working on symptoms does not stop the pain; it just masks it for a while. A thorough analysis of the cause of your stress should be an integral part of your plan to achieve what you want and desire. Removing the cause of the stress may fulfill the goal you are trying to achieve.

- *Sometimes it can be as simple as keeping faith in yourself and your plan.* Confidence in your plan and in the approach you take to achieving what you want is a form of self motivation. If you have faith in your self, it will be obvious to others that you are a motivated person. Remember that you present yourself to the world from the inside out.

- *Partnering with others to achieve your Executive Focus is possible when you are not competitors after the same goal.* Working with others in similar positions in other organizations may give you a new perspective on ways to achieve your goals. One way to do this is through involvement in a professional organization that is aligned to your long-term career plans. Most professional organizations have local chapters that meet monthly. Involve yourself with a sub-committee that works on issues central to your plan and the goals you want to achieve.

Keep yourself motivated, engaged, and pumped up. It's a tough job because it requires you to constantly have a positive approach toward life and life's many trials and tribulations. Things may not go smoothly when you start the process of re-aligning your life and career. It is a constant battle against unseen forces that affect you. Sometimes it is the luck of the draw rather than good planning that causes things to go right or wrong.

When things go right, use the experience to pull yourself up to a higher motivation and commitment level that will allow you to accomplish and achieve what you want. Pick up the pace for getting what you want. Nothing succeeds like success.

When things go wrong, do not let it pull you down. Try to stabilize your motivation level and hold the course. Do not let yourself be thrown off track. Vince Lombardi once famously said, "The best defense is a good offense." Use that philosophy and be prepared when bad things happen. Always have a contingency plan in place in case something goes wrong or gets off track. The worst de-motivation occurs when you are caught off guard and clueless as what to do next.

Remember: only you will make your Executive Focus a reality. An old saying is applicable here: you can "make something happen, watch it happen, or wonder what happened." Be one of those who make things happen. Watch all the others wonder what happened and watch them watch you succeed as you attain your career and life goals.

Index

Page numbers in *italics* refer to tables or illustrations.

A

achievement goals, 79–88
active listening, 37, 39
alignment
 organizational concept of, 13–14, 47, *49*
 personal-professional, 69–77, 79
attitude, importance of, 56–57, 77, 112, 124
audience, importance of knowing, 27, 28
avoidance goals, 79–88

B

baby boomer workforce population, 36–37, 102, 104, 112–113
balance, life and career, 135
balanced scorecard, 13–17, 19, 35
The Balanced Scorecard (Kaplan and Norton), 38
behavior and teams, 119–120
belongingness needs, 114
Blink (Gladwell), 95
business planning model, *49*
business process management (BPM), 49, 53
business tension, 64

C

career alignment, factors affecting, 72–74, *73*
career goals, 80–88
career planning, 69–70, 77
Carlson, Curtis, 56
Cashman, Kevin, 46
champions, team, 122–123
change, organizational, 29, 63, 76–77
clutter, 45–57, 92
clutter matrix, personal and organizational, 47, *48t*
coaching, executive, 65
collective resources, 54
common purpose, commitment to, 115–117, 120
communicating unmentionables, 27–28
communication, 23–32
conflict, 25, 29, 120
Core Process Redesign five-step model, 42
corporate vision, 25–26
Covey, Stephen R., 27, 57
creating momentum, 62–63
creative conflict, 120
creative tension, 64
critical organizational knowledge, 103
critical-skill employees, 109
CRM (customer relationship management), 38
cross-functional teams, 112, 118
culture of orderliness, 92
curiosity, intellectual, 36

current-state study of organizations, 41
current-state talent assessment, 104
current-worker pool, 105
customer loyalty, 37
customer relationship management (CRM), 38
cycle of awareness, 33

D

dark energy, xvi–xviii, 25, 29, 64–66, 91, 137
data, evidence-based, 13
data-based decisions, 27–29
decision making, 24–29
decisions
   communicating, 23–32
   hard *vs.* soft, 27–29
departing workers, 108
dirty work, leadership, 53–54
disenchanted workers, 107
dissociated workers, 108
DNA, organizational, 103
doubt, 4–8, *6*
downsizing, 43, 63–64

E

early warning systems, 89–99
effective groups, 120–121
effective leadership, 23, 29–30
effective teams, 113–118, *116t–117t*
emotional needs, 136–137
employee involvement, 65, 112
employee loyalty, 37, 104
employee turnover, 104
employees
   as clutter, 50–51
   critical-skill, 109
enrolled workers, 107
errors, type I and type II, 80–81, 83
essence, cultivating, 46
esteem needs, 114–115
evidence-based data, 13
executive behaviors, 37
executive challenges, 63

executive coaching, 65
executive focus, ix–x, xv–xvi, 19-21,
   and alignment, 55, 69-70
   and goals, 79–80
   and information overload, 130
   and organizational clutter, 45
   and personal momentum, 67
   and teams, 112, 125
   and transition zones, 75–77
executive focus fog, 2-3
executive library, value of, 42
executive responsibilities, 53
executive turnover statistics, xi
external balanced scorecards, 35

F

families, characteristics of successful, 121
feeling *vs.* sensing, 96–97
flocking behavior, 54
fully-engaged workers, 106–107
future-state talent requirements, 104

G

gap analysis, 104
generation X workers, 60–61, 112–113
Gladwell, Malcolm, 95
goal setting, 79–88
good stress, 29–30
growth goals, *18*
growth strategies, 18–19, 43, 63–64

H

hard data, 35
hard decisions *vs.* soft, 27–29
Harvard Business Review (Kaplan and Norton), 16–17
headcount, balancing, 50–51
hearing, filters for, 94
historic organizational knowledge, 108–109
Human Resources, role of, 44, 51, 101–110
hypothesis testing, 80

I

ideas, communicating, 23–32
individual balance points, 29
information
    failing to believe, 42
    sources of, 33–38
    sharing, 24
inner circle, 24, 29
innovation and teams, 120–125
intellectual curiosity, 36
intellectual intelligence, 35
intelligence data, gathering, 34–38
internal monitoring system, 16–17, 33
internal sensory scorecard, 35
interpersonal skills, 37
intuition, 20, 36, 95
intuitive decisions, 27–29
intuitive intelligence, 35–36

J

job-and-place mismatch phenomenon, 69–77, *71*

K

kinetic energy, 65–66

L

language of coaching, 65
leadership
    challenges, 29, 59–60, 63
    and clutter campaign, 48–54
    interpersonal skills, 33, 37
    responsibilities, 23
    rewards, 30–31
    social requirements, 25
leadership team, recognition of, 30
leading indicators, 35
lean, 66
Lean Enterprise tool, 52–53
listening, 34–38, 36–37, 65
listening, five-step model for, 39–40, *40t*
listening tours, 93
Lone Ranger school of management, 37
loyalty, employee, 37, 104

M

maintenance strategies, 42, 62, 64
management support for effective teams, 122–123
manure management, ix
Maslow's needs hierarchy, *114*
measurement systems, 87–88
mental effectiveness and physical activity, 56
mentoring programs, 109
millennial generation workers, 112–113
momentum, personal and organizational, 59–67
moray eel personality types, 11–12
motivation, generating, 137–139
multi-generational teams, 111–125

N

new world of work, 127, 135
noise, 46, 91–92

O

operational performance, measuring, 13–17
organizational change, 29, 63, 76–77
organizational clutter, 45–57
organizational DNA, 103
organizational fog, 1–8
organizational knowledge, 38–41, 108–109
organizational measures, *20t*
organizational momentum, 59–67
organizational needs, 33–44
organizational operations, 35–38

P

panic attacks, ix
passive-aggressive personalities, 9–10
performance management systems, 104–105
performance reviews, 106
personal and corporate vision, 25–26
personal avoidance goals, 83

personal clutter, 54–56
personal environment scan, 43–44
personal fog, 1–8
personal growth, 77
personal momentum, 67
personal planning model, 55
personal sacrifice, 71–72
personalities, passive and aggressive, 9
personality types, 9–12
physical activity, importance of, 29, 56
physiological needs, 114–115
planning models, *49*, 55
private doubt, 6–7
public doubt, 7–8

Q

qualitative information, 36
quantitative balanced scorecard, 35
quantitative measures, 18–19

R

rapid cognition, 95
relationships
  and effective teams, 121
  short-term, 2–4
  trusting, 34, 40
reorganization strategies, 62
report card, 16–17
restructuring strategies, 18–19
retirement drain, 102–103, 108–110
reward and recognition programs, 66–67
rewards of leadership, 30–31
risk analysis, 105

S

5s rules for reducing clutter, 52–53
sea fog, 1–2
seasoned executives, coaching role for, 61–62
secret system knowledge, 108
security needs, 114–115

self-actualization needs, 115
self awareness, 36, 38, 41–44
senior leadership
  commitment, 23, 24
  disconnect with younger employees, 36–37
  interpersonal skills, 37
  long-term and short-term strategies, 42–43, 62–63
  responsibilities and rewards, 30–31, 53
seniority empowered personality types, 10–11
sensing *vs.* feeling, 96–97
sensory indicators, 89–99, *91*
short-term relationships, 2–4
social skills, importance of, 37–38
Strategy + Business magazine, xi
stress, ix, 5, 29–30, 74, 94, 127–133
succession planning, 61–62
surfer personality types, 11
survival needs, 136
SWOT exercises, 25–26, 31

T

talent management crisis, 102–103
talent retention system, 104
teams
  culture, 112
  sponsors, 122–123
  and technology, 118–119
technology and stress, 128
technology secrets, retaining, 108
time management, 127–133
transition zones, 74–77
trust relationships, 34, 40, 57
turnover, employee, 102, 104

U

unmentionables, communicating, 27–28
unrealized achievement need, 60

V

vision, 25-26

W-X

whale personality types, 12
"what if" questions, 44
work
  enjoyment of, 30–31
  nature of, 54
worker involvement, 105–108, *106*
workforce talent, 101–110

Y-Z

yard sale, executive focus, 45–46
"yes but" answers, 44